At Home with
HENRY VIII

At Home with
HENRY VIII

His life, his wives, his palaces

ROSE SHEPHERD

CICO BOOKS

LONDON NEW YORK

Published in 2014 by CICO Books
An imprint of Ryland Peters & Small Ltd
20–21 Jockey's Fields   341 E 116 Street
London WC1R 4BW   New York, NY 10029

www.rylandpeters.com

10 9 8 7 6 5 4 3 2 1

A CIP catalog record for this book is available from the Library of Congress and the
British Library.

ISBN: 978 1 78249 160 6

Printed in China

Editor: Alison Wormleighton
Designer: David Rowley
Picture Researcher: Claire Gouldstone
Illustrator: Becca Thorne

Publishing Manager: Penny Craig
Art Director: Sally Powell
Production Director: Patricia Harrington
Publisher: Cindy Richards

For digital editions,
visit www.cicobooks.com/apps.php

CONTENTS

Introduction 6

Chapter One PASTIME WITH GOOD COMPANY 12

Chapter Two MOST HONORABLE HOUSEHOLD 34

Chapter Three GREATE AND COSTLY ARRAY AND APPARRELL 54

Chapter Four HAMPTON COURT HATH PRE-EMINENCE 72

Chapter Five POWERHOUSE, TREASUREHOUSE, SLAUGHTERHOUSE 92

Chapter Six A VERY VALLIANT TRENCHERMAN 116

Chapter Seven NO OIL PAINTING 130

Chapter Eight ABOMINABLE, BASE, CARNAL, VOLUPTUOUS 144

Chapter Nine PHYSIC AND CHIRURGERY 160

Chapter Ten A MAN OF PROPERTY 176

Resources 186

Index 187

Picture credits and acknowledgments 192

INTRODUCTION

*T*wilight. Cockshut time. Now is the hour for the ritual making of the king's bed. The Groom of the Bedchamber summons four Yeomen of the Bedchamber, he calls for four Yeomen of the Wardrobe, who bring the sheets, the embroidered silk coverings and pillows. With a Gentleman Usher, they line up to right and left, and, by the light of the Groom's torch, the ceremony begins.

First a yeoman stabs the straw repeatedly with a dagger, to be sure "that there be no untruth therein." Once the mattress is laid over it, another yeoman rolls and tumbles on it, "for the search thereof," before the solemn, synchronized spreading of the sheets and counterpanes, the smoothing of the pillows, the making of the sign of the cross upon them, and the dropping of a kiss on the spot where His Grace will lay his great head.

Henry VIII lived in a style almost unimaginable today. His father had left him a vast fortune built on swingeing taxation—and a vast fortune Henry would spend, on futile foreign wars and extravagant buildings. Prestige, privilege, and the constant aspiration to "magnificence," the determination to outshine his French and Spanish rivals, drove him relentlessly as he descended, over a reign of almost 38 years, from a handsome, cultured Renaissance prince said to have "no wish for gold or gems or precious metals, but virtue, glory, immortality," to a bloated, avaricious, vengeful, self-pitying despot, physically, mentally, and emotionally wrecked.

His court was a heaving mass of nobility, servants, and the servants of servants. It was a place of pageantry, profligacy, and display, of whispering conspirators, fawning sycophants, performers and posturers, nobles and retainers. How oppressive, corrupting, and ultimately dementing this was we shall see as we move through his life and his marriages to six strikingly different women. It is little wonder that he loved to chase deer, to ride out with the wind in his face, to be free for hours from the panoply of state and the claustrophic atmosphere of the court.

By looking at the pastimes he enjoyed, the sports at which he excelled, the style he affected, the food he ate, the palaces he acquired, furnished, and embellished, the arts he encouraged, the ailments he endured, and not least the minutiae of his day-to-day existence, we come to know and understand the man more fully.

Fascinating glimpses are afforded by the records of the royal privy purse expenses. There we find "playing money" for Henry's insatiable gambling habit. Noted, too, are payments of alms, gifts, endowments. Purchases of jewelry, finery, bows and arrows, candlesticks, lute strings, riding caps, greyhounds, horses, a cello, a hawk glove, hose for the king's Fool, "a bonnet trimmed with ribbon and a dog chain"… Disbursements for services include those for "washing of his shert and other necessaryes," for trimming his barges, for ferrying him between his palaces, for a sermon at Lent, to the King's Apothecary, to the Keeper of the Windsor Armoury, to the Keeper of the Clock at Hampton Court, to stable boys, falconers, gardeners, minstrels. Among sundry rewards are those made for bringing a sturgeon, lampreys, apples, strawberries, a mastiff, a red deer, a buck, "grene geese," rosewater from Guildford, a hogshead of wine, artichoke, pomegranate, six messes of meat, hens, snuffers, hobbies, a fox. There are gratuities, also, for "the Mayor of London for bringing cherries to my lady Anne," for "the men of Staines for bringing a salmon," and, touchingly, to one unknown "for bringing home Ball, the King's dog, lost in the forest of Waltham."

On the darker side, there is this from November 1530: "Item. My lord fferrers 6l 13s 4d for taking of a Trayto." Would that be Walter Devereux, Lord Ferrers, chief justice of South Cymru? And the traitor, the rebellious Rhys ap Gruffydd, whose titles and properties Henry had bestowed upon Devereux? A Catholic, friend of Katharine of Aragon and no fan of the king's ladylove Anne Boleyn, Rhys was beheaded in 1531 on flimsy charges of attempting to overthrow Henry and declare himself Prince of Wales. His widow was the firebrand Catherine Howard, a daughter of the 2nd Duke of Norfolk. Her half-brother, Thomas Howard, 3rd Duke, was the uncle of both Anne Boleyn and

Kathryn Howard. Those two unfortunate queens and first cousins would meet the same fate as Rhys. Thomas Howard would be condemned for being party to his son Henry Howard's alleged plan to snatch the throne—though not before he had sentenced both Anne Boleyn and her brother George, his niece and nephew, to die. He outlived the king and was eventually freed by Queen Mary, but Henry Howard went to the scaffold. Just a handful, then, of the tens of thousands to be executed in Henry VIII's reign.

Welcome to the world of Bluff King Hal.

We three queens

The spelling of the forename shared by three of Henry's wives is arguable—and hotly argued. Henry's Spanish wife, princess of Aragon, was christened Catalina, justifying the popular use of "Catherine." However, she signed herself "Katherina" and took a "K" for her monogram, so we are favoring "Katharine," as it appears writ large in gilded lettering on her tomb in Peterborough Cathedral. Henry's sixth wife, styling herself variously though assuredly "Katherina Regina KP" and "Kateryn the Quene Regente KP," will be "Katherine Parr," while the pathetic young fifth queen, with her less declamatory, more immature and smudgy "Katheryn," is here "Kathryn Howard." None is absolutely right or wrong, but choices have to be made, and it seems important to distinguish them from one another.

TIMELINE

Katharine of Aragon

Anne Boleyn

Jane Seymour

August 2, 1485	Henry Tudor defeats Richard III at Bosworth Field to seize the crown as Henry VII.
December 16, 1485	Catalina (Katharine) born to "the Catholic kings" Isabella of Castile and Ferdinand of Aragon.
January 18, 1486	Henry VII marries Elizabeth of York.
September 20, 1486	Birth of Prince Arthur.
November 28, 1489	Birth of Princess Margaret Tudor.
June 28, 1491	Birth of Henry, Duke of York, at Greenwich Palace.
March 18, 1496	Birth of Princess Mary Tudor.
November 14, 1501	Marriage of Prince Arthur and Katharine of Aragon.
*c.*1501–1507	Anne Boleyn born at Blickling, Norfolk.
*c.*1508	Birth of Jane Seymour.
April 2, 1502	Arthur dies at Ludlow Castle.
February 11, 1503	Elizabeth of York dies from postnatal complications; the girl child did not survive the birth.
April 21, 1509	Death of Henry VII; Henry VIII ascends the throne.
June 11, 1509	Henry marries Katharine.
June 24 1509	Coronation of Henry and Katharine.
*c.*1512	Birth of Katherine Parr.
September 22, 1515	Birth of Anne of Cleves.
February 18, 1516	Birth of Princess Mary.
*c.*1523	Birth of Kathryn Howard.
1527	Henry explores the means to annul his marriage.
1529	Cardinal Wolsey fails to persuade Cardinal Campeggio to annul Henry's marriage. The case is referred to Rome. Wolsey falls from grace.
November 29, 1530	Wolsey dies at Leicester on his way to London to stand trial for treason.
1531	Henry declares himself head of the Church of England.

Anne of Cleves

Kathryn Howard

Katherine Parr

January 25, 1533	Henry secretly marries Anne Boleyn.
May 23, 1533	Henry's marriage to Katharine annulled by Thomas Cranmer, Archbishop of Canterbury.
May 29, 1533	Anne Boleyn is escorted by barge from Greenwich Palace to the Tower of London; the coronation celebrations begin.
June 1, 1533	Anne is crowned queen.
September 7, 1533	Birth of Princess Elizabeth.
1534	Pope Clement VII rules that Henry's marriage to Katharine was valid. Henry introduces the Act of Supremacy; he appoints Thomas Cromwell controller of the Church.
June 22 & July 6, 1535	Execution of John Fisher and Sir Thomas More for refusing to recognize the king's religious supremacy.
1536	The Dissolution of the Monasteries begins.
January 7, 1536	Death of Katharine of Aragon.
May 19, 1536	Anne Boleyn is executed.
May 20, 1536	Henry is betrothed to Jane Seymour.
May 30, 1536	Henry marries Jane Seymour.
October 12, 1537	Birth of Prince Edward, the future Edward VI.
October 24, 1537	Jane Seymour dies.
December 27, 1539	Anne of Cleves arrives at Dover.
January 6, 1540	Henry marries Anne of Cleves.
July 1540	Marriage to Anne of Cleves dissolved.
July 28, 1540	Thomas Cromwell, marriage broker, executed; Henry marries Kathryn Howard.
February 14, 1542	Execution of Kathryn Howard.
July 12, 1543	Henry marries Katherine Parr.
January 28, 1547	Death of Henry.

Chapter One

PASTIME WITH GOOD COMPANY

"Every heart smiles to see its cares dispelled, as the day shines bright when clouds are scattered. Now the people, freed, run before their king with bright faces. Their joy is almost beyond their own comprehension. They rejoice, they exult, they leap for joy and celebrate their having such a king. 'The King' is all that any mouth can say."

From Thomas More's Coronation Ode of Henry VIII

It is May Day morning, a day for fertility rites, for pagans to make a mighty clamor to wake up tardy spring. It is the anniversary of the death of Robin Hood and is consecrated to him. The queen is in her chamber with her ladies when that legendary outlaw of Sherwood Forest bursts in. Behind him surge eleven of his Merry Men, all hooded, in short coats of Kendal green, brandishing bows and arrows. They perform several dances and then depart. Amid the hilarity and feigned shock, there is no mistaking the true identity of Robin, the folk hero, Lord of Locksley. Who else at court but the young king stands an inch over six feet and cuts such a dash?

*H*enry is full of the joys of spring. He delights in his masques, mummery, and maying, he delights in his japes and "disguisings," but above all he delights in his Spanish wife.

Katharine of Aragon is such a little thing, yet strong-minded, highly educated, clever, pious, pleasingly plump, and fair. Henry writes to her father, King Ferdinand II, that if he were free he would choose her again. His union with the widow of his elder brother, Arthur, is ordained by the Bible (Deuteronomy 25:5): "If brethren dwell together, and one of them die, and have no child… her husband's brother shall go in unto her, and take her to him to wife." It is a marriage, indeed, made in heaven. And Henry is convinced it is written in the stars that his queen will bear him sons.

There are two things that everyone knows about Henry VIII—he was hugely fat and he had six wives ("divorced, beheaded, died, divorced, beheaded, survived" goes the familiar folk rhyme). Most might add that he split with Rome, appointed himself Supreme Head of the Church of England, dissolved over eight hundred religious houses and grabbed their lands, hanged disobliging abbots at their gates, and wreaked appalling vengeance on those who dissented from his view or failed to achieve his ends.

It is history's punishment for Henry that the abiding image of him is of a degenerate monster. But it wasn't meant to be that way. When the tall, vigorous, cultured, deeply religious, affectionate Henry, Prince of Wales, ascended the throne in April 1509, at not quite 18, he had high hopes and aspirations. After the repressive, extortionate regime of his father, it was as if the sun had risen over a benighted realm. "Heaven smiles, earth rejoices, all is milk and honey and nectar," as the courtier William Blount, 4th Baron Mountjoy, wrote to Erasmus of Rotterdam. "Avarice has fled the country.

:H·R· ·AŇ·ETATIS
VIII: XXXV:

Our king is not after gold or gems, or precious stones, but virtue, glory, immortality."

No one, least of all the king himself, would have foreseen, upon that dawn, the total eclipse of the young Henry by the old. If only we had one really telling portrait of the princely paragon, to hold at least a pale candle to the later depictions of the swaggering plutocrat! What we do have is a word picture from Thomas More's coronation ode, describing the "fiery power in his eyes, Venus in his face, the colour of twin roses in his cheeks." His visage, "admirable in its animated strength," could have been equally that of a man or a maiden.

As to the jubilation and hero worship sweeping the land, "Every heart smiles to see its cares dispelled… Now the people, freed, run before their king with bright faces." The staunchly Catholic More went on to serve as a councillor and later Lord Chancellor to Henry. On July 6, 1535, he was beheaded at the Tower of London. He was to have been hanged, drawn, and quartered, but the sentence was commuted by the king—the very king who More in his coronation ode had said would "wipe the tears from every eye and put joy in the place of our long distress."

🐦 A star is born

Henry's story begins on June 28, 1491, with his birth at the Palace of Placentia in Greenwich, southeast of London. He was the third child and second son of Henry VII and the gentle, nurturing Elizabeth of York. Of

BELOW: *Lost in the mists of time: the vanished Palace of Placentia on the river at Greenwich, Henry's birthplace, where he married Katharine of Aragon. A favorite residence, it was the scene of unbridled revelry.*

ABOVE: *The dedication page from the 1502 horoscope for the royal family prepared by Italian astrologer Gulielmus Parronus, known as William Parron. For the future Henry VIII, Parron predicted a happy marriage and numerous male heirs. Wrong!*

their seven offspring, only Arthur, Margaret, Henry, and Mary would survive childhood. While his father groomed Arthur for kingship, Henry, Duke of York, grew up with his sisters. His paternal grandmother, Lady Margaret Beaufort, managed his domestic arrangements and supervised his education, while he learned at his mother's knee to read and write. He had first-class tutors, among them the poet laureate John Skelton. He was schooled in literature, rhetoric, Latin, Greek, French, Italian, mathematics, and, not least, theology, in preparation for holy office and eventually the see of Canterbury.

Because the Tudors set store by astrology, we may note that though Henry was born under the sign of Cancer, at his nativity the sun stood in notoriously contrary Gemini, while his rising sign was Leo—on the one hand confident, cultivated, noble, proud, and irrepressible, and on the other hand overblown, intolerant, self-justifying, and impossibly demanding.

Not that you can always trust an astrologer. Consider Gulielmus Parronus, known as William Parron, a "physician and professor of astrology," imported from Italy to the court of Henry VII, where he was author of the first almanac to be published in Britain. Anxious to find favor with his new master, in 1499 he presented the king with a document entitled *The Fateful Meaning of the Stars*. In it he cited the conjunction of Jupiter and Saturn to justify Henry Tudor's seizure of the throne from Richard III at Bosworth Field, giving succor to the shifty usurper. In 1502, upon the death of Prince Arthur, he got to work on a similarly ingratiating horoscope. In *The Book of the Excellent Fortunes of Henry Duke of York and his Parents*, he predicted for Henry a life of religious devotion and a happy marriage blessed with abundant male issue. Elizabeth of York, he confidently foresaw, would live to 80. Upon her death, aged 37, in February 1503, Signor Parronus slipped away from court, never to be heard of again. Even so, Henry VIII would cling to his fictions, and, lo, they were coming true! The life of religious observance, the bliss of a loving marriage… With the birth of the promised sons, Parronus's claims for the "ineluctable power of the stars" would be vindicated.

⚘ Arthur and after

The loss of his elder son and of his wife within less than a year of each other may in some part explain Henry VII's state of mind in his declining years, but it would take more than the adverse alignment of planets to excuse his treatment of his daughter-in-law, Katharine of Aragon.

Many of his problems stemmed from insecurity. A Welsh-born Lancastrian, he had a tenuous claim to the crown he had won in battle. The Yorkist Elizabeth, by contrast, was a Plantagenet, the daughter of Edward IV and elder sister of Edward V. Her uncle, the Duke of Gloucester—long believed to have murdered young Edward and his brother Richard, the "Princes in the Tower"—had been crowned Richard III but then vanquished at Bosworth by her future husband. Elizabeth wed Henry VII early the following year, uniting the houses of York and Lancaster, bringing to the marriage not just royal blood, but emotional and psychological ballast. The betrothal had been arranged by Henry Tudor's mother, the indefatigable intriguer Lady Margaret Beaufort, but he entered into it with a full heart. This was well for him, since love was never a consideration.

Like it or not, their daughter Margaret was to marry James IV of Scotland. Mary was promised to Charles of Castile, although she would instead eventually be hived off by her brother Henry to Louis XII of France. Most crucially, to secure a powerful ally in Spain, Henry VII negotiated a deal for his elder son and heir. Arthur, Prince of Wales, was born on September 20, 1486, at least a month premature if he was conceived in wedlock. He was betrothed in infancy to Catalina (later called Katharine), youngest child of Isabella I of Castile and Ferdinand II of Aragon, architects of the Spanish Inquisition.

Catalina had been born on December 16, 1485, and by the time of her marriage to Arthur at the Norman cathedral of St Paul's in London on November 14, 1501, these two young people had already been twice wed by proxy, with the Spanish ambassador standing in as bride. The British adored the Spanish princess, with her creamy skin, rosy cheeks, and red-gold hair. The ten-year-old Prince Henry, escorting her at the spectacular wedding

ABOVE: *Henry's elder brother, Arthur, was born at Winchester, the legendary King Arthur's Camelot. He was 15 when he married Katharine of Aragon, only to die a few months later.*

OPPOSITE: *Demure and deeply religious, Katharine had so little time to get to know her young husband. Their intimacy—or otherwise—would become a mortifying matter of public scrutiny.*

ceremony, can have been no less enamored. Wine fountains on the streets added to the good cheer. The partying continued for two weeks.

Arthur and Katharine spent their wedding night at the palace of the Bishop of London, and what did or did not happen behind the closed doors of the bedchamber, nobody knows. In the morning Arthur was in high spirits. "Willoughby," he called to his steward, "bring me a cup of ale, for I have been this night in the midst of Spain." And, later, "Masters, it is a good pastime to have a wife." However, this may just have been bravado, because when Henry married Katharine eight years later, he bragged that he took a maiden to the marriage bed (a claim that would come back to bite him). It is entirely possible that Katharine's first marriage was not consummated. Arthur was a fragile youth, even shorter than his diminutive wife. In his portrait, the eyes of a child look out from a face that would never resolve itself into the firm lines of manhood.

In April 1502, at Ludlow Castle, he and Katharine both fell ill with what was probably the sweating sickness. This "most pitiful disease… cruel and fervent enemy of nature," which was presaged in the sufferer by a sense of dread, was so virulent that it could carry away the victim within hours. Arthur, weakened by earlier illness, died. Katharine recovered, to find herself widowed at 16, as Prince Henry found himself, overnight, heir to a kingdom.

Following Arthur's death, there was some consolation for Henry VII and Elizabeth when she almost immediately conceived their seventh child. But neither she nor the baby girl survived, as within nine days of the birth Elizabeth had succumbed to what may have been puerperal fever. The king had lost his wife, Prince Henry had lost his beloved mother, and Katharine of Aragon had lost the support of the woman who might have saved her from the ignominy that followed. For, while her father-in-law and father spent years wrangling over dowry, paid and unpaid, she was by turns betrothed to Prince Henry then repudiated. The treaty of betrothal was signed in June 1503. But two years later, on the eve of his 15th birthday, Prince Henry was made to denounce the contract signed in his minority, declaring it null and void. In all this time, Katharine was kept in the meanest circumstances, confined with her caviling Spanish household, shuttled between palaces, and—though they were often under the same roof—denied contact with Prince Henry, whom she persisted in calling her "husband." A princess twice over, daughter of two reigning monarchs, she wore shabby clothes, sold off her treasures, went hungry, and was reduced to pleading with her papa to part with what he owed of her marriage portion.

OPPOSITE: *Henry's mother, the kind, gentle, conscientious Elizabeth of York, was the daughter of Edward IV. Her untimely death left Katharine at the mercy of her manipulative and avaricious father-in-law.*

Most repulsive of all was the English king's plan to marry her himself. He had promised Ferdinand that he would be a "second father" to the princess, but for a while he toyed with the idea of becoming, instead, her second husband.

A portrait of Henry VII, attributed to the Flemish artist Michael Sittow, shows him aged 48, a sly fox, small-eyed, his few black teeth concealed by thin, pursed lips, with a red rose in his hand and unmistakably something up his sleeve. It was painted by way of advertisement for another prospective bride, Margaret of Austria, Duchess of Savoy, the daughter of Maximilian I, King of the Romans. One imagines that Margaret found the face unsympathetic; she made it very clear that she would sooner remain a widow. And although our perception may soften slightly when we recall that the king was ravaged by consumption, handsome Prince Henry effortlessly outmans him in the mind's eye.

On April 21, 1509, at Richmond Palace, Henry VII breathed his last, and his successor burst upon the scene like a meteor shower. For Katharine the nightmare was over. Her prince rode to the rescue, raised her up, enthroned her at his side. On June 11, 1509, at Greenwich, in a private ceremony, Henry and she were married, and on Midsummer's Day, at Westminster Abbey, she shared in his coronation. She was now aged 23. He was not obliged to marry her. There were younger, prettier, more generously dowered princesses on offer to him. The fact is that he *chose* Katharine. Like his father before him, Henry VIII married his heart's desire.

✎ Reveling in it

The difference between the court of Henry VII and that of Henry VIII was in some degree the difference between the optimism of youth and the crankiness of infirm age. Henry VII was not without culture. He had a fine library and welcomed scholars, such as the humanist Erasmus of Rotterdam. He gave his children every educational advantage.

Richmond Palace, the "Rich Mount," which he built on the site of the old royal manor at Sheen, with its river frontage, its many windows and minarets, courtyards and galleries, formal gardens, fountains and statuary, was an "earthly and second paradise… the lantern spectacle and beauteous exemplar of all lodgings." The extravaganza staged for the wedding of Arthur and Katharine had been two years in the planning. There were revels in the old king's reign, there was music and dance, and he gambled like a demon. But his suspicious nature and the spies in his pay—his "flies and familiars"—made for a wasps' nest atmosphere, while serial bereavements, failing eyesight, and tuberculosis were heavy burdens for him personally to endure.

OPPOSITE: *The bereaved Henry VII wasted no time in seeking a new wife, but Michael Sittow's portrait of him, clutching the red rose of Lancaster, symbol of love, failed to enchant his prospective bride. The image, though not life-size, is as realistic as it is unappealing. Around his neck he wears the Order of the Golden Fleece, calculated to impress his European peers.*

Anno 1505 20 octobis ymago henrici vii trancie rege illustissimi ordinata p hermann zinck Ro regie ... ... illustium · ...

In this illustration the Latin text reads:

Xultate Deo adiutori nostro
iubilate Deo Iacob
umite psalmum: & date tympanum
psalterium iocundum cum cythara .

ABOVE: *In grand state rooms and his private chamber, Henry always had music. In this illustration from his psalter, a quartet plays the dulcimer, harp, drum, and horn. Written and illuminated by Jean Mallard, a French emigré scribe, calligrapher, and king's poet, the psalter has been heavily annotated in Henry's own hand.*

By contrast, for Henry VIII, assured in his kingship, heir to a stable realm and overflowing coffers, this was a glad confident morning. "Our time is spent in continuous festival," wrote Katharine to her father.

Music was central to life at court, providing a backdrop to leisure, repasts, and state occasions, and reinforcing royal prestige. Henry employed some 60 musicians, recruiting them from France, Italy, and the Netherlands, as the English court orchestra aspired to outplay the rest of Europe. The king's tastes had been shaped in boyhood by the lutenist Gilles Duwes, who had taught him French, and who remained his friend in adulthood. The Venetian organist Friar Dionisius Memo was sent over from St Mark's by the doge in 1516 to become Henry's chaplain and choirmaster. Of all the king's pleasures, wrote the Venetian ambassador, "is always Memo's music… The King is so enamoured of him and pleased with his talent that one could not wish for more."

William Cornysh, composer, poet, and actor, was Master of the Children of the Chapel Royal (the choirboys). Much later, Thomas Tallis, "the father of English cathedral music" and the most important home-grown composer of his day, would enter court service as a Gentleman of the Chapel Royal.

As well as public concerts, Henry would summon to entertain him in his private quarters musicians such as the keyboard player Benedictus de Opicijs, from Antwerp, and Philip van Wilder, a Netherlandish lutenist and Keeper of the King's Instruments. In later years they were joined by Mark Smeaton, a young and handsome singer and dancer, doomed, in 1536, to join a most wretched quintet (see page 108).

The king not only loved to listen to music and to sight-read, but was also an accomplished musician, fond of playing the lute, harpsichord, and bagpipes. He had recorders, flutes, trumpets, and trombones by the dozen in van Wilder's care. Among nearly 40 part songs and instrumental pieces that he composed was one entitled "Pastime with Good Company," also known as "The King's Ballad," expressing the belief that "youth must have some dalliance." It reads like a manifesto for unbridled fun and games:

ABOVE: *Henry was a gifted composer. The 20 songs and 13 instrumental pieces, collected in* The Henry VIII Songbook *in around 1518, are still performed today. The exuberant "Pastime with Good Company" captured the national mood and became a popular hit of its day—reprised in 2007 by Jethro Tull on acoustic guitar.*

Pastime with good company
I love and shall until I die
Grudge who will let none deny
So god be pleased this life will I
For my pastance hunt sing and dance
My heart is set
All goodly sport for my comfort
Who shall me let.

ABOVE: *As well as his lifelong passion for deer-hunting, Henry loved to hunt with birds of prey, such as the beautiful gyrfalcon. A hawking glove preserved at Oxford's Ashmolean Museum may have been the king's own. Designed to protect the hand from a raptor's talons, the doeskin right-hand glove is embroidered with silver and gilt thread, and colored silks.*

Hunting, hawking, singing, dancing were but a few of those goodly "pastances" (pastimes) for Henry's pleasure. At court there were games of tennis, bowls, archery with longbow and crossbow, hare-coursing, cockfighting and bear-baiting, tilting at the quintain, and running at the ring. Henry was an ace at tennis (the old game we now call "court tennis" or "real tennis"). In 1522 he partnered the Holy Roman Emperor Charles V against the Prince of Orange and the Marquis of Brandenburg, a match of eleven games that ended, somehow or another, in a draw.

Under the law, many sports were the preserve of the court élite. In 1512, tennis, bowls, skittles, and games of cards and dice were banned for ordinary mortals. The shockingly violent game of football, beloved of young male commoners—a free-for-all played with a ball stuffed with dog hair, between goals a mile apart—would eventually be banned in 1540. Being "more a fight than a game," it too often resulted in punch-ups, knifings, and broken necks and limbs among the nation's youth, who might be required to take up arms.

The king also had his Fools, both "natural"—with some physical or mental impairment or pure insanity—and "artificial," to act the fopdoodle, clowning around for him. His long-time favorite was Will Somers, whose stoop must have made him a natural, but who would cut capers, crack jokes, and tell riddles with the best of the artificials. Somers had license to voice the kind of cheeky remarks that would have got others into deep trouble. The king ("Harry," to his Fool) and Will had great fun with games of "tag rhyming," spouting improvised verse and trying to cap one another.

Betting was an obsession. The Tudor weakness for gambling was in Henry's blood, and he expected his nobles to wager large sums, accepting their losses with equanimity. He would bet on Tables (a form of backgammon), Bragg (a precursor of poker), Queek (a sort of checkers), Ruff, Noddy, Post and Pair, Put or Putt, and the outcome of a tournament, a horse race, a dog fight, a shooting contest. It is said that his losses at cards ran to £3,250 over one two-year period. He even bet the bells of Jesus Chapel in St Paul's churchyard on the roll of the dice—and lost. The courtier Sir Miles Partridge, who had staked an astronomical £100, duly removed the bells for melting down, and demolished the timber bell tower.

Most reckless of all, Henry gambled a large part of the wealth that his father had so assiduously husbanded, on vanity-driven military adventures in France. He failed to distinguish himself on the battlefield, but achieved the warrior status he craved back at home as a champion of the joust. This

RIGHT: *In this illustration
from his psalter, Henry
appears with his favorite
court Fool, Will Somers, who
was close to the king for more
than 20 years. The image
accompanies Psalm 52, "The
fool says in his heart, 'There is
no God.'" As elsewhere in the
psalter (see page 45), Henry is
represented as King David,
here playing the harp.*

potentially lethal sport, which would be the death of the French Henry II,
provided the perfect platform for bravura and a show of medieval chivalry.

A letter from the Venetian ambassador's secretary, in May 1515, describes
how "this most serene King made his appearance in very great pomp: on his
side were ten of these noblemen on most capital horses, all with housings of
one sort, namely, with cloth of gold with a raised pile, His Majesty's war horse
being likewise caparisoned in the same manner; and in truth he looked like
St George in person on its back." The joust on that day lasted for three hours
to the accompaniment of trumpets and drums, "the King excelling all the
others, shivering many lances, and unhorsing one of his opponents."

Christmas, Twelfth Night, Epiphany, Shrovetide, Eastertide, St George's
Day, May Day, Whitsun, Corpus Christi, Michaelmas… no occasion could
go unmarked by celebration. The Revels Office dealt with far more than
drafting in jesters, jugglers, tumblers, dwarfs, giants, and high-wire walkers.
A veritable army of set builders, carpenters, scene painters, poets, musicians,
choreographers, designers, embroiderers, and seamstresses would be employed
to create stunning spectacles for masques and pageants. Reverential reports by
foreign dignitaries mention bowers of songbirds, arbors decked with flowers
and sweet herbs, and "cars" (chariots) pulled by griffins with human faces.

ABOVE: *A painted roll at the College of Arms in London recalls the day when a jubilant Henry challenged all comers to joust in an allegorical tournament. He styled himself "Noble Heart" as he rode before Katharine, "Queen of Noble Renown." The event was a celebration of the birth of a son and heir.*

However, it is the accounts of Richard Gibson, Master of the Revels until 1522, that provide the most vivid and amusing picture. From these we learn that as early as January 1510 work was under way upon the Robin Hood costumes for Henry's May Day surprise—including a dress for "a woman like Maid Marian," in which role a pageboy was cast. The long and detailed accounts speak of doublets for minstrels, ostrich feathers, robes and bonnets for two Turks, 48 gold pomegranates, boat hire, "6 white velvet bonnets for lords disguised… 118 lbs. orsade for flossing and casing the lion… Spanish brown for colouring the beasts… 3 coifs of Venice gold, for the maiden in the forest, and those that rode on the lion and the olyvant… Gold for gilding the antelope's horns… verdigris for colouring moss and ivy leaves… ½ bushel of wheat flour for paste for covering 'gargells faces and small serpents that garnschyd founten'… satins and sarcenets… for the apparel of 28 lords and ladies and 6 minstrels…", girdles for mummers, aprons for painters, bells for the dancers and knights… and so on, and on, and on.

The masques had such titles as "The Rich Mount" (a play on "Richmond"), and "Venus and Beauty." Typically, women were portrayed as imprisoned and isolated; male dominance was a recurring theme. "Le Fortress Dangerous," devised by Cornysh, featured a castle in which sat six ladies, besieged by Henry and his courtiers.

Traditionally, masques had been performed by professional disguisers as the prelude to dance. Now, however, costumed courtiers represented allegorical themes, such as Riches and Love, their knights sparring for supremacy—with the king and queen either actively engaged or present both as spectators and, symbolically, as players.

On New Year's Day, 1511, a year after she was delivered of a stillborn girl, Katharine gave birth to a longed-for boy. On January 5, he was christened Henry, and in mid-February days of tournament and revels of an unprecedented splendor were staged at Westminster. Katharine, "Queen of Noble Renown" of the "Kingdom of Noble Heart," was declared to have sent the bold knights

Coeur Loyal, Bon Voloir, Bon Espoir, and Valiant Desire (Henry and three of his courtiers) to take on all comers. To spectators it must have appeared that Birnam Wood had come to Dunsinane, as the challengers arrived inside a mobile forest crowned by a castle of golden paper. Gibson's accounts for that jamboree run to hundreds of items and read like an orgy of extravagance.

Ten days later, baby Henry was dead.

✍ Behind the masque

The death of the king's first-born son was but one sobering aspect of the tale. The fact is that what might appear superficially to have been an endless round of sybaritic indulgence was driven by a far more earnest agenda.

Magnificence, magnificence, magnificence. Always and in everything Henry must show the world what he was made of—and what he was made of, principally, was money. When visiting royals and aristocrats were wined and dined in style without precedent, when ambassadors and diplomats, frequent guests at Henry's entertainments, returned home with tales of the glories of England, or wrote in dispatches of the wonders of the court of King Henry, it would be seen that he had no equal. From splendiferous palaces, mighty castles, gold and silver plate, down to gold and silver dice, everything had to be *par excellence.*

The flaunting of affluence would reach its apotheosis in 1520 when, amid scenes of superabundance, for two and a half weeks in June, Henry met with Francis I outside Ardres near Calais, England's last possession in France, at what became known as the Field of Cloth of Gold. Temporary palaces, banquet houses, and pavilions were erected, and Henry's tent was indeed of cloth run through with gold filament. Each king had some 500 horsemen and 3,000 foot soldiers. At the outset the two men's legions stood stock still and silent, on pain of death, facing each other across the valley, as Francis and Henry rode down to embrace. There followed festivities and days of tournament, with contests in wrestling and archery. Music organized by William Cornysh entailed the French and English Chapels Royal, in a purpose-built chapel, singing in alternation at a service.

Henry's sense of rivalry with his "dear brother of France" was keenly felt and personal as well as political. Talking with Sebastian Giustiniani, the Venetian ambassador, in 1515, upon the accession of Francis, he had pressed him: "The king of France, is he as tall as I am? Is he as stout? What sort of legs has he?" On being told that there was little difference in height, that Francis was not as stout, and that his legs were thinner, Henry unfastened his doublet, placed his hand on his thigh and bragged, "Look, here! And I have a good calf to my leg." At Ardres, still feeling he had something to prove, in defiance of the agreed protocol he challenged Francis to a wrestling match—and was beaten. Cornysh promptly penned a three-part song for Katharine, commemorating Henry's courageous endeavor.

The two kings had vowed perpetual friendship between their countries, but it rested upon a handshake. Two years later, on June 16, 1522, at Windsor Castle, Henry and Charles V, the Holy Roman Emperor, were to sign the Treaty of Windsor, forming a military alliance against France. Charles's arrival was marked by a procession that included two bulls and a dragon, "whiche beastes cast out fyer continually."

The entertainments included, apart from tennis, two days of hunting and a play by Cornysh in which Francis I was represented by a wild horse, bridled by Amity, Prudence, and Might.

The Field of Cloth of Gold might be seen as surrogate warfare, with each of those vain kings determined to best the other, or, as is often suggested, it could be interpreted as a gigantic sham. Henry was no stranger to cynical posturing, the first instance of which came within days of his accession. In 1510, as he danced for his wife in the guise of Robin of the Greenwood, two men languished in the Tower of London while charges quite as creative as their own tax-collecting methods were worked up against them.

In a shrewdly calculated crowd-pleasing gesture, Henry had hauled before the Privy Council his father's trusted extortionists Richard Empson and Edmund Dudley—"the king's long arms with which he took what was his." Loyal if egregious servants to Henry VII, they had been, wrote Francis Bacon in his 17th-century histories, "like tame hawks for their master, and like wild hawks for themselves, insomuch as they grew to great riches and substance."

For their sins, which were many, although not strictly capital offences, they were charged with "constructive treason" and sentenced to public execution, which was carried out in August 1510. Their informers, or "questmongers," were rounded up and "rode about the city with their faces to their horses' tails and papers on their heads, and were set on the pillory on Cornhill, and after brought again to Newgate, where they died for very shame."

It was a masterstroke of propaganda. The message to the people was clear—the king understood their grievances against those agents of the crown, the "ravening wolves, horseleeches and shearers" who had worked so hard to impoverish them.

The people were heartily thankful, in their honeymoon delirium, to be rid of old Henry. Time would show, however, that new Henry was after all no Robin Hood.

ABOVE: *The Field of Cloth of Gold was an orgy of extravagance and ostentation. For two and a half weeks in June 1520, Henry and the French king, Francis I, with their vast entourages, were encamped near Calais, in France, feasting, jousting, and pledging perpetual friendship. It was all too good to last.*

Chapter Two

MOST HONORABLE HOUSEHOLD

"The wealth and civilization of the world are here; and those who call the English barbarians appear to me to render themselves such. I perceive here very elegant manners, extreme decorum, and very great politeness; and among other things there is this most invincible king whose acquirements and qualities are so many and excellent that I consider him to excel all who ever wore a crown."

Letter from Francesco Chieregato, the papal nuncio, to Isabella d'Este in 1517

On June 15, 1519, Henry became the father of a healthy boy. Christened Henry FitzRoy ("son of the king"), the child was destined at age six to become the Duke of Richmond and Somerset—although never to ascend the throne.

OPPOSITE: *The boy who might have been king: Henry FitzRoy, born in June 1519. Henry VIII showered his illegitimate son with titles and honors, but any plans that he made for him were thwarted by Fate. FitzRoy's tomb is at St Michael's Church, Framlingham, Suffolk.*

Queen Katharine had been a staunch wife. In 1513, rising to the challenge of regency while Henry was waging war in France, she had taken delivery of a lead coffin containing the embalmed body of James IV of Scotland, the king's upstart brother-in-law, killed at the Battle of Flodden. She had sent Henry the Scottish king's slashed and bloodied coat, urging him to use it as a banner. (Her original plan, to send James's disemboweled body, had been vetoed by her advisers, for "our Englishmen's hearts would not suffer it.")

On February 18, 1516, she had borne him a daughter, Mary, his "pearl," but five other pregnancies had resulted in the stillbirth or early death of three boys and two girls. At the age of 30, she was physically broken—"old and deformed," as Francis I, already father of one surviving daughter and two sons, coarsely mocked. Even if Henry had still desired her, there was no question of another child.

Meanwhile, in 1512 there had come to court from Kinlet, in Shropshire, John Blount—a relative of William Blount, 4th Baron Mountjoy, the queen's Chamberlain. John Blount served first as one of the King's Spears, and later in the privileged position of Esquire of the Body, a member of the select team whose job it was "to array the king and unarray him, and no many else was to set hand upon the king," to convey to the Yeomen of the Body "all the king's stuff… and to take charge of the cupboard at night."

John's daughter Bessie was 12 or 13 when she began to move in court circles, as a maid of honor to Katharine. She first appears in the records on May 8, 1513, when the court accounts at Greenwich record a payment to her of an annuity of a hundred shillings. But it is in the records of the Christmas revels at Greenwich in 1514 that Bessie comes vividly alive. Richard Gibson's accounts show, among four female participants, "Maysteres Elisabeth Blont." The ladies were robed in gowns of white satin lined with blue, with mantles and bonnets of blue velvet, and coifs of gold-piped damask. All were beauties, but Bessie stole the show, for it is recorded that the "damosel, in singing, dancing, and all goodly pastimes exceeded all other." To the king, weary of lumpen, aging Katharine, disappointed of a male heir, this vivacious, nubile blonde was irresistible.

ABOVE: *Sir Thomas Boleyn was a brilliant linguist, jouster, and diplomat. With Elizabeth Howard of that great Norfolk dynasty, he had three children who survived childhood, Mary, Anne, and George. He projected a dazzling future for his offspring, but two of the siblings were destined for the executioner's block.*

They embarked on a liaison that ended after the birth of Henry, proof that the king could sire a boy ("Bless 'ee, Bessie Blount," the wags wisecracked). It is possible that Bessie also gave the king a daughter, called Elizabeth, but Henry FitzRoy was the only illegitimate child he ever acknowledged.

Among the other players on Richard Gibson's list for those Christmas festivities, certain names resonate, such as "Mayster Sir Thomas Bollyn" and his brother "Mayster Edward Bollyn." Ennobled by Henry VIII at his coronation, Thomas Boleyn was another Esquire of the Body, so he was in a very real sense close to the king. He was a linguist and a man on the make, destined to become a brilliant ambassador, heading the negotiations for the Field of Cloth of Gold. He would need to be socially adroit as Henry moved on from blessed Bessie to Boleyn's elder daughter, Mary, before Mary's younger sister, Anne, arrived to turn his head. Whether Henry also "had to do" with the girls' mother, Lady Elizabeth, is conjecture.

Like Bessie, Mary Boleyn was a maid of honor to Katharine, as was Anne from 1521. Gossip had it that both Boleyn sisters had been mistresses of Francis I, a legendary goat. Rodolfo Pio da Carpi, who in the mid-1530s was the papal nuncio at the court of Francis I, albeit with an axe to grind, dismissed Mary as "a very great whore, the most infamous of them all."

In the year of Henry FitzRoy's birth, Erasmus wrote to the courtier Sir Henry Guildford, extolling the marriage of Henry and Katharine: "What household is there among the subjects of their realm that can offer an example of such united wedlock? Where can a wife be better matched with the best of husbands? Nowhere could be found so pure and modest a Court." Guildford, as Master of the Horse and an Esquire of the Body, naturally knew better. As a friend of Henry's, naturally, he kept his counsel.

It was not so outrageous for a king to have mistresses—if anything it was expected. In France the chief mistress traditionally enjoyed the status of *maîtresse en titre*. Henry's first known affair was in 1514, with the French Jane Popincourt, his sisters' former language tutor. But, against the background of disillusion and disaffection, the court of Henry VIII appears not "pure" or "modest" as Erasmus claimed, but, beneath the veneer of decorum, seedy and malignant, a breeding ground for jealousy and paranoia.

☙ The world at his feet

When he ascended the throne, Henry inherited numerous royal residences, to which he would add compulsively throughout his reign. Between Eltham Palace, east of London, and Windsor Castle to the west, he would travel by royal barge to the Palace of Placentia in Greenwich, the royal apartments in the Tower of London, the medieval Baynard's Castle near St Paul's, Bridewell Palace at St Bride's, the Palace of Westminster, and his father's stupendous creation at Richmond.

When Westminster Palace was partially destroyed by fire in 1512, it remained the seat of government, but Greenwich became Henry's preferred headquarters. The "court" was not, however, vested in one building, but in the king with his teeming, scheming entourage, wherever he might be. His household—in some winters well over one thousand strong—was a rapacious

RIGHT: *On the waterfront at London's Blackfriars stood turreted Baynard's Castle, on the site of a 14th-century tower of the same name. It was transformed into a royal residence by Henry VII, and Henry VIII made a gift of it to Katharine of Aragon. Charles II would dine there before it was consumed by the Great Fire of London in 1666.*

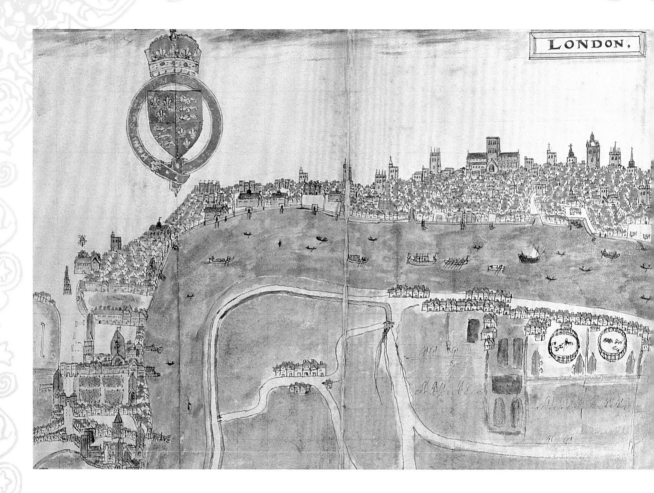

consumer of goods and services, fuelling the economy, keeping builders,
carpenters, jewelers, goldsmiths, mercers, clockmakers, chandlers, tanners,
tailors, hosiers, and dozens more in constant industry. In 1517, a joust in
honor of a Flemish ambassador, featuring harnesses of pure silver, kept all the
smiths in London busy for four months.

Only the inexhaustible tidal waters running through the city rivaled the
royal court as an employer and engine of prosperity. The Thames was far more
than a winding thoroughfare between palaces—it was the lifeblood of the
capital. Tudor London (population 60,000 in 1509) was not raised up above
it; buildings crowded on its banks. On the single medieval bridge were
clustered houses, churches, and shops. (You can to this day pass through the
medieval pedestrian entrance archway, part of the fabric of the church of
St Magnus the Martyr.) On any morning the residents might be brought up
short by the sight of traitors' heads displayed on poles.

The bridge's multiple narrow arches reduced the salinity of the water,
causing it to freeze at higher temperatures. The river was also wider and

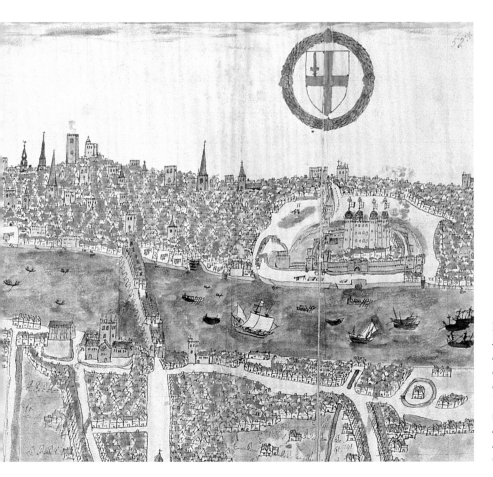

LEFT: *The river provided a safe and convenient conduit between the royal residences of London and Henry's outlying palaces. Father Thames brought wealth and industry to the capital. It was a gateway through which the luxuries of the known world were borne to the king.*

slower-moving in Henry's time and the winters were colder (the era is now referred to as the Little Ice Age), so the Thames would freeze over at times. Henry was once able to reach Greenwich by sleigh.

Londoners lived on the river, worked on it, traveled on it, profited from it. It was thronged with the domestic traffic of barges, lighters, and ferries, rocking in the wake of oceangoing trading ships, for this was the gateway to the world with all its treasures, debouching into the "Broade Ditch" of the Channel, across which lay Calais. Henry was creating a major maritime, military, and mercantile nation. Downriver went British merchant ships laden with blue broadcloth from Colchester, linsey-woolsey from Worcester, hops and beer from Kent. Downriver, too, went battleships from the new royal docks at Woolwich and Deptford.

Upriver came galleys and carracks bearing exquisite Venetian glass, saffron and cloth of gold, rice from Genoa, wine from Gascony, silks from Lucca, fustian from Naples, eye-glasses from Florence, linen from Ghent. They brought woad from Toulouse, sugar and cork from Oporto, soap from Castile;

ABOVE: *Not for nothing did Henry fear the traitorous assassin. When he traveled, he took with him his locksmith to secure his bedchamber. This ornate lock, wrought for him, is retained at Hever Castle, once home to Anne Boleyn.*

leopards for the royal menagerie, Andalusian jennets, Neapolitan coursers, and Flemish "roiles" (draft horses) for the king's stud; little white dogs from Malta; five sets of sables courtesy of Charles V; a hundred Damascene carpets from the Levant, a gift to a certain influential cardinal from the merchants of Venice; Spanish satin and majolica; live eels, almonds, oranges; rats and other stowaways—and the great pox of Naples, aka *peste de Bordeaux, gorre de Rouen*, or "the French disease."

Christopher Columbus, on his voyages between 1492 and 1503, sponsored by Henry's future mother-in-law, Isabella, had exported smallpox to the Americas and imported syphilis to Europe, where it was spread by armies on the move. Some experts have attributed Henry's mental instability in later life to the infection, though modern historians tend to discount this. Exotic disease as well as all the luxuries of the known world arrived by water at King Henry's doorstep.

⚘ The great royal roadshow

What a strange beast was the court of Henry VIII, a shape-shifting, ravening, untamable, itinerant behemoth! Surrounding it was a notional "verge," an area within defined boundaries or a radius of 12 miles from wherever the king was resident. It was under the authority of the Lord Steward—from 1540 known as the Lord Great Master.

In summer Henry and a heaving retinue would set off on a "progress," to meet the landed gentry, to discover his kingdom, to dazzle his subjects, and to invite them to pay homage. Descending upon towns and cities, he would make a "royal entry" to be met by local dignitaries, amid scenes of pageantry

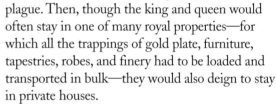

and rejoicing. He would hear "the complaints of the poor commonality" and be called upon to settle disputes, but he missed no opportunity to hunt, dance, sing, and joust.

The baggage train clattered and rumbled from place to place, with horses, wagons, mules, and an army of courtiers, soldiers, sappers, and servants from all departments, including Henry's locksmith to secure his bedchamber against would-be assassins. Along went the merry multitude, chasing stags, hawking, fishing, littering, soiling, trampling, and kicking up dust. Wherever the court touched down it was as if a plague of locusts had landed. Once resources were drained to the dregs, it moved on, leaving a scene of devastation for others to make good.

An itinerary, or "giest," for a progress would be drawn up in advance, bearing in mind such considerations as the condition of roads and possible outbreaks of plague. Then, though the king and queen would often stay in one of many royal properties—for which all the trappings of gold plate, furniture, tapestries, robes, and finery had to be loaded and transported in bulk—they would also deign to stay in private houses.

There was no greater kudos than to play host to the sovereign, and it was deemed to be well worth the crippling expense. Nicholas Poyntz was not unique in so desiring to impress Henry when he received him at Acton Court in Gloucestershire, that he built an entire new wing to accommodate him. He bought in glass from Venice and majolica from Spain, sparing no expense, and was rewarded with a knighthood on the spot.

The strategy was not without hazard, given the king's tendency to acquire any house on which he had his beady eye. When he was entertained by the 3rd Duke of Buckingham at Penshurst Place in Kent in 1519, the Duke lavished more than £1 million in today's money on a feast for him, arousing suspicions in the king's mind as to his host's ultimate ambitions. In 1521 Buckingham was beheaded for treason and his medieval manor was forfeit to the Crown. It made a very agreeable hunting lodge

ABOVE: *Henry was not always a grateful guest. The 3rd Duke of Buckingham, Edward Stafford, spent a fortune improving Penshurst Place in Kent and entertaining the king in 1519. Two years later, on Buckingham's brutal demise, the house passed to the Crown—in the person of Henry.*

for Henry, happily close to Hever Castle, Thomas Boleyn's country seat, and to Anne.

Three times Henry stayed at The Vyne in Hampshire, once with Anne, as guest of his Lord Chamberlain, William Sandys, 1st Baron Sandys of The Vyne—making, one imagines, for some awkwardness when eventually it fell to Sandys to escort the queen on her final journey to the Tower.

Good housekeeping

Nothing apart from war, it was said, was more disruptive to the order and well-being of court life than a summer progress. Even when not on the road, it was logistical hell. From the reign of Edward IV, the *Liber Niger* (Black Book) had set down in minute detail the principles of management for the royal household. The duties of every noble and court officer were defined, along with their allowances for food, pitchers of wine, gallons of ale, candles, torches, faggots, rushes, livery, pay, perquisites, and permissible numbers and rank of servants. From Bishop Confessor, Chancellor, and Great Chamberlain to knights, chaplains, keepers of the wardrobe, gentleman ushers, Esquires of the Body, yeomen, grooms, physicians, heralds, harbingers, pursuivants, sergeants-at-arms, criers, standard-bearers, waiters, minstrels, messengers, and scullions, everyone had designated rights and responsibilities.

The system was theoretically highly structured, disciplined, and bureaucratic, but the reality was organized chaos. Within the two main departments of the *Domus Regis*, the King's Household, hundreds of waged servants were granted "bouge of court," the right to eat at the king's expense. The *Domus Providencie*, the "below stairs" division, with a staff of some 200 to 250, was responsible for the provision of food, drink, fuel, and other necessities. The *Domus Magnificentie*, front of house, was responsible for maintaining the image of princely splendor and largesse.

While it sounds the more costly, the *Domus Magnificentie*, under the Lord Chamberlain, was relatively manageable. It was the *Domus Providencie* that was always out of hand. This was the domain of the Lord Steward, the Treasurer, the Controller, and the Cofferer, with the "Board of Greencloth," or Counting House, dispensing money to sub-departments. It had the

impossible task of reconciling demands for economy with the ceaseless requirement for magnificence. Budgeting was a nightmare, with fluctuating numbers of visitors and ambassadors to be assimilated, and with a king whose whim might call for lavish hospitality without notice. To exacerbate the problems, certain nobles—deaf to minstrels "blowing and piping" on "trumpesses, shalmuse and small pipes" to summon them to table— dispatched their servants to fetch food from the kitchens to consume in their own quarters, delighting to "dine in corners and secret places" while their allotted rations went untouched. The extravagance, waste, and scope for abuse were on a monumental scale, and serial attempts at reform were thwarted.

Above stairs, communal meals were taken in the Great Hall or Chamber, scene of public business, ceremony, feasts, and revels. Beyond this was the Presence Chamber, in which Henry would receive important guests. And beyond that again was the Privy or "Secret" Chamber, Henry's private apartment, with bedchamber, withdrawing room, "tiring room," closet, and other amenities. The Privy Chamber was a fiefdom, out of bounds to all but a privileged élite. As the doors were kept at all times by ushers, grooms, and pages, the exclusiveness was keenly felt by those who found these doors closed against them.

The queen's accommodation was similar to the king's, but smaller. The royal couple could live quite separate lives, which, increasingly, Henry and Katharine did. While this once-vaunted "united couple" nursed their own heartbreak, they drifted apart. By the time she was 40, Katharine had more or less withdrawn from the frivolity, finding solace in religious devotion, while Henry, at 34, continued to partake of scintillating court life.

🖋 Sundry errors and misuses

The gross entitlements of kingship did, of course, come with responsibilities, in particular for patronage, which Henry was honor-bound to confer upon those who could convince him. New Year's Day was traditionally the occasion for petitioners to make their approaches, but all year round the courtiers vied for the king's attention.

Political success no longer depended on nobility alone. Aristocrats could not count solely on their bloodline for preferment. Men of a different stripe were on the rise, gifted and able individuals chosen for their intellect. A commoner of good education and with the determination to succeed could hold the highest office.

Thomas Wolsey, the son of a Suffolk butcher and cattle dealer, had attended Magdalen College, Oxford, before his ordination, entering the household of Henry VII in 1507. His humble background had stood him in good stead, as the old king strove to rein in the nobility. In 1509 Wolsey was appointed almoner (distributor of alms for the poor) to the new king, rising to become, in short order, Dean of York, Bishop of Lincoln, Archbishop of York, a cardinal—and, by December 1515, Chancellor of England. As Henry's first Chief Minister, he was in control of the institutions of power and justice.

Thomas Cromwell, son of a Putney blacksmith, trained in law and worked his way up from Privy Councillor to King's Chief Minister, Lord Privy Seal, and Earl of Essex.

Both would come to sorry ends, but while the going was good these men got going. In the autumn of 1525, Wolsey devised for Henry the Eltham Ordinances, 79 chapters of meticulously drafted regulations "for the establishment of good order and reformation of sundry errors and misuses in his most honourable household and chamber."

OPPOSITE: *A genius of statecraft, though with a weakness for luxury and a penchant for display, Cardinal Wolsey was tireless in his work for Henry. Wolsey's head, said his biographer and Gentleman Usher, George Cavendish, "was full of subtle wit and policy." He basked in "fortune's bliss" and the king's favor—until his fall from grace.*

CARDINAL WOOLSEY

Everything in court, down to wine lees and spent candles, was to be accounted for. Thus, "no wax, white lights, wood nor coals more than reasonable ought to be spent by the overnight gentleman ushers," while the groom porters were "to daily bring in the remain of the torches and other wax remaining overnight, by nine of the clock in the morrow"—one week's wages to be docked for every failure to comply.

Against a background of institutionalized filching and squandering, the ordinances bristled with warnings. Discipline, prudent budgeting, and scrupulous accounting were stressed. Bouge allowances, for eating at the king's expense, were reduced. Theft even of household furnishings was evidently rife, since this was severely indicted.

Henry's preoccupation with good hygiene was reflected in the following extract from the Eltham Ordinances:

And for the better avoiding of corruption and all uncleanness out of the King's house, which doth engender danger of infection, and is very noisome and displeasant unto noblemen and others repairing unto the same, it is ordained by the King's Highness that the three master cooks of the kitchen shall have each of them by way of reward yearly twenty marks, to the intent they shall provide and sufficiently furnish the said kitchen of such scullions as shall not go naked or in garments of such vileness as they now do... nor lie in the nights and days in the kitchen or ground by the fireside..."

The "relicts and fragments" of food and drink—the leftovers from the king's and queen's chambers and household—were to be distributed to poor folk at the outer court gate, under the supervision of the almoner, "without diminishing, embezzling or purloining any part therefore."

The character, competence, and integrity of household officers and servants were implicitly impugned:

... to the intent the King's Highness may be substantially served in his chamber and household by such personages as be both honest in their gesture and behaviour, and also expert in such rooms and offices as be deputed unto them; considering also the great confusion, annoyance, infection, trouble, and dishonour that ensueth by the numbers as well of

sickly, impotent, unable and unmeet persons, as of rascals and vagabonds, now spread, remaining and being in all the court…

Sickly and unmeet persons? Rascals and vagabonds? Who on earth could he have meant?

❧ The minion mafia

If we return to the revels at Greenwich at Christmas 1514, where Bessie Blount made such a stellar impression, we find listed two further significant names—those of "Nicholas Karew" and "Maysteres Karew the young wyff."

Nicholas Carew had been in Henry's household from age six, rising to become a prominent courtier. So skilled and fearless at the joust was he that Henry granted him his own tiltyard at Greenwich. Carew was variously Master of the Horse and Master of the Forests, Lieutenant of Ruysbank Tower, guarding Calais, and the king's Chief Esquire. His "young wyff," Elizabeth, was the sister of fellow courtier Sir Francis Bryan. It was rumored of Elizabeth Bryan that she had been another of the king's mistresses. Both Carew and Bryan were among the few admitted to the inner sanctum of the Privy Chamber, unsuitable though they were for such an honor.

In 1509 Henry had drafted in four of the men who had served him as Prince of Wales, to attend him in his Privy Chamber. William Compton, William Thomas, William Tyler, and John Sharp were appointed as grooms, Compton to the most coveted role of Groom of the Stool and Senior Gentleman of the Privy Chamber.

Compton was, by the nature of his work, more intimate with the king than any other individual, since it was his job to attend him upon his "close stool"—his latrine, a box padded with black velvet, which opened to reveal a pewter bowl beneath a hole in the center. What confidences the two shared while Henry relieved himself, those on the outside could only imagine. Compton no more felt degraded by the menial task than Henry minded the want of privacy. He was public property and rarely alone. When, much later, his physician, Dr Butts, gave testimony as to his "nocturnal emissions" at the

BELOW: *Henry stayed several times at redbrick Compton Wynyates in Warwickshire, seat of his most intimate servant, William Compton, Groom of the Stool. Compton died of the sweating sickness in 1528 and is buried here in the chapel.*

hearing to annul Henry's marriage to Anne of Cleves, the physician did not cross a line of propriety but confirmed that the virile king still had what it took to father a child.

Like Carew, Compton had been at court since boyhood as a ward of the Crown, acting as a page to Prince Henry. As his groom he now had charge of the king's jewels and bed linen. Among the other services he is said to have rendered was the procurement of women. Whether this was so or not, Henry was sufficiently appreciative to make a gift to him of ruined Fulbroke Castle, which Compton cannibalized for *spolia* for his Warwickshire stately home, Compton Wynyates, including a bay window of heraldic glass and many mullioned windows with vine-pattern ornament. Several times Henry visited him there.

As well as the four grooms, Henry could admit others, such as chaplains and physicians, at will, to his Privy Chamber. There was, too, a second group of men, his "minions"—*mignons,* favorites, cronies, jousting companions—whom he liked to have around him. In the early days these were men some ten years older than he was, valued for their maturity and experience. But from 1513 men younger than Henry, such as Bryan and Carew, basked in his affections.

On occasion, minions would be sent by the king as emissaries abroad. In France, those reprobates Carew and Bryan so hit it off with Francis I that the three of them went on the rampage, in disguise, as they "rode daily through Paris throwing eggs and stones and other foolish trifles at the people." On returning to England, they were way above themselves, "all French in eating, drinking and apparel. Yea, and in French vices and brags, so that all the estates of England were by them laughed at, the ladies and gentlewomen were dispraised."

In May 1519, at Wolsey's behest, the King's Council called for the dismissal of "certain young men in his Privy Chamber [who], not regarding his estate nor degree, are so familiar and homely with him, and play such light touches with him, that they forgot themselves." Carew and Bryan were summoned by the Lord Chamberlain, "with divers also of the Privy Chamber which had been in the French court," and banished. It was not the first time that these obnoxious upstarts were removed, before inveigling their way back into the fold.

With his Eltham Ordinances, Wolsey's private agenda was to reduce the number of gentlemen, the grooms and minions keeping company with the king, and to neutralize the power of the Privy Chamber. His concern was not so much with the moral fiber of licentious brats as with the influence wielded by that particular cabal. They were perfectly placed to advise Henry on patronage, promoting the interests of some, scuppering the hopes of others. Catching Henry in a good mood, they could slide forward papers for signing—in a bad mood, he would sign nothing—and could even, with impunity, forge his signature, a cursive "HR" formed by one flowing motion of the pen. "He sayth the kynge doth wryte,/And writeth he wottish nat what" as Henry's old tutor, the poet John Skelton, derided (digging, actually, at Wolsey), suggesting that Henry would inattentively put his name to and set his seal upon documents he had not read. By his own confession he detested all paperwork.

How Wolsey must have tossed and turned at night as he thought of Compton and the minions, all hugger-mugger, as they poured venom into the king's ear! How he resented Compton—and how Compton resented Wolsey!

The Ordinances relating to the Privy Chamber amount to a thoroughgoing condemnation of laxity, sloth, squabbles, and grudges. The pageboys were to rise at a surprisingly late seven o'clock to make the fire and wake the esquires, who should be up and dressed and ready before eight. "Moreover, that none of the servants of the said esquires for the body come within the pallet chamber, but be attendant at the door." At the esquires' command the pages were to "fetch in and bear out the night gear, and all other their clothing…" Six gentlemen were to be up at seven—or sooner if the king decreed it, "in the said chamber there diligently attending upon his Grace coming forth, being ready and prompt, to apparel and dress his Highness, putting on such garments, in reverent, discreet and sober manner, as shall be his Grace's pleasure to wear." No groom or usher should "approach or presume… to lay his hands upon his royal person, or intermeddle with preparing or dressing of the same."

The king's barber was to be on hand with "water, cloths, knives, combs, scissors, and such other stuff as he needs, for trimming and dressing the king's head and beard." He was to "take special regard to the pure and clean keeping of his own person and apparel, using himself always honestly in his conversation, without resorting to the company of vile persons, or of misguided women, in avoiding such dangers and annoyance as by that means he might do unto the king's most royal person."

The stipulations called for the disputatious Privy Chamber inmates to be "loving together, and of good unity"; there must be close-mouthed discretion, and in Henry's absence they "shall not only give their continual and diligent attendance in the said chamber, but also leave asking where the king is or is going, be it early or late, without grudging, mumbling, or talking of the king's pastime; late or early going to bed…"

Most crucially, "It is the king's pleasure that Mr Norris shall be in the room of Sir William Compton, not only giving his attendance as groom of the stool but also in his bedchamber and other privy places as shall stand with his pleasure."

So Norris was in and Compton was out—of the Privy Chamber, at least. But Wolsey was not an outright winner. For courtiers in the reign of Henry VIII, life was a fraught game of Snakes and Ladders.

The chamber staff of 22 was to be cut to six gentlemen, including Sir Henry Norris, two ushers, four grooms, a page, and the barber. The eight to be paid off included Carew and Bryan. But by 1528 the diabolical duo were reinstated, Bryan minus one eye, lost in a joust, and wearing a patch. By 1530 the numbers had crept back to 20, with a further eight joining by 1538.

In 1538, Carew was finally to overreach himself, talking back to Henry, and allegedly conspiring to depose him. On the committee that judged him guilty sat his old friend Bryan—"the Vicar of Hell," as Thomas Cromwell dubbed him. Carew was destined to be beheaded on March 3, 1539, leaving his wife Elizabeth, Bryan's sister, in penury. Norris had by then already met a similar end.

To Compton and Wolsey, fate would be been slightly kinder. Sir William Compton died in 1528, of the sweating sickness. Of Wolsey's downfall we shall read anon.

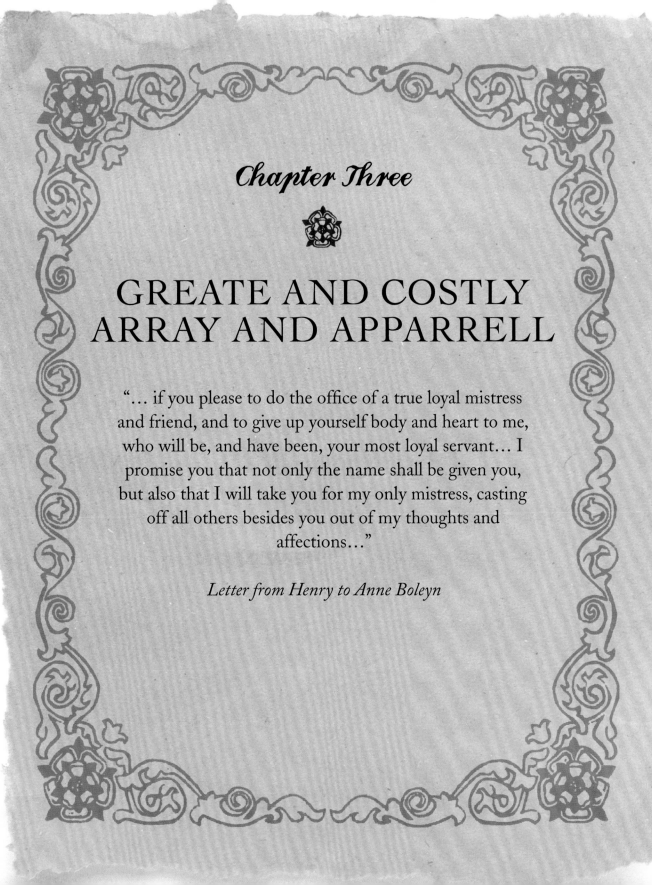

Chapter Three

GREATE AND COSTLY ARRAY AND APPARRELL

"… if you please to do the office of a true loyal mistress and friend, and to give up yourself body and heart to me, who will be, and have been, your most loyal servant… I promise you that not only the name shall be given you, but also that I will take you for my only mistress, casting off all others besides you out of my thoughts and affections…"

Letter from Henry to Anne Boleyn

"The king… wore a cap of crimson velvet, in the French fashion, and the brim was looped up all round with lacets, which had gold enameled tags. His doublet was in the Swiss fashion, striped alternately with white and crimson satin, and his hose were scarlet, and all slashed from the knee upwards. Very close round his neck he had a gold collar, from which there hung a round cut diamond, the size of the largest walnut I ever saw, and to this was suspended a most beautiful and very large round pearl… and his fingers were one mass of jeweled rings."

Trust an Italian, a citizen of the republic of Venice, to have such an eye for sartorial detail. This was the doge's ambassador Sebastian Giustiniani, who was always grandiloquent in his praise for the king, describing how he appeared on St George's Day at Richmond with his Knights of the Garter.

"Nature could not have done more for him," Giustiniani related in 1519. "He is much handsomer than any other sovereign in Christendom; a great deal handsomer than the King of France." Giustiniani went on to give another hint of an insecurity—even of an inferiority complex—in Henry's preoccupation with the French king: "On hearing that Francis I wore a beard, he allowed his own to grow, and as it is reddish, he has now got a beard which looks like gold."

Elsewhere we hear from Giustiniani of "the most Christian King" dressed in "a robe of cloth of silver, with a raised pile, and figured with very beautiful flowers, the lining being of Spanish herons' feathers, which are much used here, and very expensive; and his doublet was of very costly cloth of gold; he had no crown on his head, or anything but his usual cloth cap." Another time, "His Majesty was dressed in a cap of gold tissue, slashed all over with knots, and the lining was of silver brocade."

The Esquires of the Body had not so much to dress Henry as to furnish and upholster him, embellishing his garb in a manner suitably opulent, right down to the tiniest particular. He was in every sense a piece of work. His appearance in court was the apogee of style, which his nobles could emulate only to a point, since Henry had the first choice of new and gorgeous imported textiles and jewels, and because dress was governed by statutes.

At his first parliament, in January 1510, Henry had helped to devise "An Act against Wearing of Costly Apparrell." It drew upon the model of laws passed by the preposterously vain Edward IV in 1463 and 1483, which,

among other things, had banned cobblers from making "piked" shoes with pointed toes of more than two inches.

Further Acts were to follow in 1514, 1515, and 1533, refining the dress codes even more. One laudable aim was to discourage the use of imported fabrics at the expense of English cloth merchants. Another was to dissuade young men from spending more than they could afford, and resorting to crime: "Forasmuch as the greate and costly array and apparel used within this realm contrary to good statutes thereof made hath been the occasion of impoverishing of diverse of the king's subjects and provoked many of them to rob and do extortion and other unlawful deeds to maintain thereby their costly array."

However, by ostentatiously swagging themselves in furs, fine textiles, and classified colors, the king and his nobles could also assert their lofty status over the rising mercantile classes. Thus, "no person, of what estate, condition, or degree that he be, use in his apparel any cloth of gold of Purpure [purple] colour but only the King, the Queen, the King's Mother, the King's children, the King's brothers and sisters upon pain to forfeit the said apparel"—which offence also incurred a fine of £20 (around £9,000-£10,000).

No man ranking lower than a duke was to use cloth of gold tissue upon his person or his horse. None lower than an earl might wear sable. And none beneath the estate of baron could use "cloth of gold or cloth of silver tinselled, satin nor no other silk or cloth mixed or embroidered with gold or silver." You had to be at least a lord or a Knight of the Garter to wear "any woollen cloth made out of the Realm of England, Ireland, Wales, Calais or the Marches of the same or Berwick," or "in gown or coat or another of his apparel any velvet of the colour of crimson or blue."

Velvet riding coats, marten's fur, damask, camlet (fabric of woven silk and goat hair), crimson or blue velvet, scarlet, crimson, or violet grain cloth, gold chains or bracelets, were all subject to restrictions, right down to the ranks of

"servants of husbandry, shepherds and labourers", who faced three days in the stocks for wearing hose priced at more than ten pennies a yard. By 1533 rules embraced gold chains, gold rings, gilt buttons, imported garters, and the furs of lynx, squirrel, civet, and black coney. At court, ushers were empowered to confiscate offending garments and to collect fines, which were split between the Lord Chamberlain and the king.

There was an awful lot of clothing to police, with all those layers, worn partly against the frigid air in the cavernous stone chambers of palace and castle. Tapestries with their allegorical depictions were more than colorful and instructive decorations; they helped to cut the cold. But even so, and despite roaring fires, courtiers shivered.

There was nothing new or particularly English about Henry's "sumptuary laws," which had been enacted across Europe since antiquity. But Henry's legislation focused on men, whereas in Renaissance Italy female dress was the target, and women developed many wiles to avoid prosecution, such as the ladies of Venice wearing studs in place of buttons, or the belles of Florence passing off ermine as the fur of "suckling" or "milky beast."

The four Acts that the king so heartily endorsed were a means of reinforcing not only class but also the male hierarchy. Women, deriving their status from fathers and husbands, were part of the structure and were expected to acquiesce. The emphasis on male finery, however, was surely a reflection of Henry's own narcissism, a love of costume inherited from his maternal grandfather, Edward IV, and the absolute imperative to set himself above everyone.

Broad padded shoulders and an exaggeratedly large codpiece played up masculinity. The outline was square. Upper and nether hose showed off the strapping legs in which Henry took such pride. Outer garments were ornamented with gems and embroidery, quilting, and brocade. It pleased Katharine to sew and embroider Henry's shirts herself. She popularized blackwork, or "Spanish work," intricate, lacy patterned stitching of black silk on white or pale fabric. Furs Henry had in abundance. Decorative slashing—slits at artful angles—afforded glimpses of more garments beneath, the under-layers sometimes pulled through the slits, or "puffed." Henry's soft caps, worn at an angle, were yet more vehicles for fur trim, feathers, and precious stones. A 17th-century commentator wrote of Hans Holbein's portrait of Henry that the spectator felt "abashed, annihilated in his presence."

In this way, Henry VIII contrived to be literally every inch a king. If he was not, as was claimed, "the best-dressed sovereign in Europe," he was certainly among the *most* dressed. Compared with the Italian-inspired elegance and more muted palette favored by Francis I, he looked like a gaudy overstuffed sofa.

As for Queen Katharine, in a later portrait, a miniature by Lucas Horenbout, she appears humorless and purse-mouthed—and who can wonder? The pretty little princess who danced the *Jota Aragonesa* has hung up her castanets and reads her Bible. Katharine, aged 40, is no match for the young, beguiling Mistress Boleyn.

ABOVE: *A miniature of Katharine of Aragon, attributed to Lucas Horenbout, shows her, in 1525, much changed since her girlhood: heftier, matronly, and faintly forbidding.*

🖎 Queen of style

Anne Boleyn was born in the early years of the new century, at Blickling in Norfolk. Her exact age cannot be told. As a girl she became a maid of honor to the Archduchess Margaret in the Netherlands, then, with her sister, Mary, to Henry's younger sister, also Mary, the "French Queen" of the feeble Louis XII. After Louis's death in 1515, Anne remained in attendance to Francis I's queen, Claude, before being recalled to the English court, to attend Katharine.

Anne was not a beauty by the standards of the day. She was a dark-skinned brunette in a society that idealized fair hair, blue eyes, and a pale complexion. Beyond that, reports of her looks diverge as widely as assessments of her character. Her detractors spoke of disfiguring moles, a goiter, a projecting tooth, six fingers on her right hand. Nicholas Sander (aka Slander)—an Elizabethan recusant Catholic, one of her most vituperative critics—wrote on hearsay that she was "rather tall of stature, with black hair, and an oval face of a sallow complexion," though allowing that she was "handsome to look at, with a pretty mouth."

RIGHT: *In his drawing of Anne Boleyn, on a rose-tinted ground, Hans Holbein the Younger illuminates our understanding of Henry's passion for his mistress. Her dark eyes are striking, and her gable hood frames an appealing face.*

To Lancelot de Carles, secretary to the French ambassador, she was "*belle et de taille elegante*" (beautiful and with an elegant figure), while in the balanced view of the Venetian envoy she was "not one of the handsomest women in the world. Of middling stature, swarthy complexion, long neck, wide mouth, bosom not much raised"—her eyes, however, were "black and beautiful." George Wyatt—grandson of the courtier poet Sir Thomas Wyatt, who was reputed to be one of Anne's desolated suitors—wrote of her: "In this noble imp, the graces of nature graced by gracious education, seemed even at

ABOVE: *A portrait in oils of Anne Boleyn in high collar and tiara hangs in the Musée Condé in Chantilly, France. She has the same dark eyes and long nose as depicted by Holbein but not the same essence. This was probably painted posthumously.*

the first to have promised bliss unto her aftertimes." He went on to say that she had a "noble presence of shape and fashion representing both mildness and majesty." Those supposedly repugnant moles were but "light motes in so bright beams of beauty."

What none can deny is that Anne Boleyn had presence and female allure. Among the charges laid against her by Henry when he would be rid of her was that she used "sortilege and charms" to bewitch him—and so, in her way, she did. Tilting her dark eyes at him, withholding her favors, showing a lively humor or a flash of her infamous temper, she had him sighing like a furnace, writing woeful ballads to her eyebrow. Women were sick with jealousy of her. Tudor ladies adored clothes, and in the matter of fashion the king's sweetheart could queen it over them—even queen it over the queen—like no other.

Her years in the sophisticated French court had shaped her style, to which she brought individual flair. She had regal bearing and danced with grace, her head held high on that slender neck. The French hood that she favored over the less becoming English "gable" hood became emblematic of her. We learn from Sander that she was "the model and the mirror" to the ladies at court, "and every day she made some change to the fashion of her garments."

What follows from Sander is a farrago of sheer calumny, supposition, and fact:

At fifteen she sinned first with her father's butler, and then with his chaplain, and forthwith was sent to France... [At the French court] she was called the English mare, because of her shameless behaviour; and then the royal mule, when she became acquainted with the king of France... On her return to England she was taken into the royal household, and there easily saw that the king was tired of his wife. She also detected... how much the king was in love with herself... The more the king sought her, the more she avoided him, sanctimoniously saying that nobody but her husband should find her alone; nevertheless she did

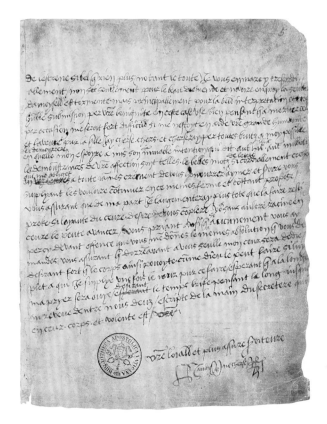

ABOVE: *For the sake of her reputation, Henry sent Anne Boleyn from court, but wrote her letters of love and yearning. He signed himself "Your loyal and most assured Servant," "Your loving Sovereign and Friend," "votre seul HR." He vouchsafed "Written with the hand which fain would be yours," and he encircled her initials with a heart.*

not think there was any want of modesty in talking, playing and even dancing with the king.

In other words, she encouraged Henry *just so far*, rejecting his advances, holding him in her thrall, as 17 of his surviving love letters, written in French and undated, attest. All these from a man who was loath even to sign his name.

For seven years or so before their short marriage, Anne was queen at least of Henry's heart, upstaging the dowdy but determined Katharine. From the privy purse records we have glimpses of Anne's glamorous, burgeoning wardrobe, for which the besotted Henry paid out royally at the height of their amours:

Shooting glove for lady Anne, 23s. 4d… 9¾ yards of crimson satin for my lady Anne, at 16s. a yard… To a Frenchman, for 6 dozen bowge skins [budge: lambs' pelts], of which lady Anne had 1 dozen… To Adington, the skinner, for furs and furring for my lady Anne's gowns, … To John Skut, for making apparel for lady Anne… 12 yards of black satin for a cloak; black velvet for edging… 16 yards of green damask… black satin for a nightgown… taffeta, velvet and buckram… crimson cloth of gold…

This is more than a mere narrative of profligate spending and a passion for fine clothes. It tells, between the lines, of power dressing on an audacious scale. Black was the most difficult color for dyers to achieve, very pricy, and much sought-after by royalty. John Skutt was the queen's tailor. How galling for Katharine that Henry should have him make fine clothing for his "other woman"! Anne, in turn, threw a tantrum when she learned that Katharine was still sewing Henry's shirts, castigating a Gentleman of the Privy Chamber who had been sent to take linen to the queen for that purpose.

In November 1529 we find: "Paied to Cecill for a yerde and a quarter of purpill vellute for mistres Anne." The Master of the Robes was ordering

velvet for Anne, in the color of royalty. Already, in her mind, she wore the crown.

The look that Anne carried off with such panache is one that has never lost its appeal—that flattering square neckline, the narrow waist, the abundant folds of fabric billowing outward, the long trains to glide and susurrate across stone floors. Over scrupulously laundered linen were layered a smock, a kirtle, and a gown displaying the usual exquisite workmanship. Flowing sleeves and under-sleeves were garments in their own right. Splendid embroidery run through with threads of silver and gold and gemstone trim were among those little touches that she bespoke. To such an ensemble would be added ostentatious jewelry—including the rubies, diamonds, and other priceless stones that Henry would command the queen to relinquish. Katharine kept back only a small gold cross and a splinter of the True Cross, which, one feels, would not have been much coveted by the woman the queen scorned as "the scandal of Christendom."

ABOVE: A gilt-bronze clock, believed to have been a gift from Henry to Anne Boleyn on the morning of their marriage. Surmounted by a leopard holding a shield emblazoned with the Royal coat of arms and Garter, it would tick away her "thousand days."

Another Henry in the field

Anne should have married Henry Percy, son of the 5th Earl of Northumberland and a descendant of the legendary Harry Percy, Shakespeare's "harebrained Hotspur, govern'd by a spleen." A member of Cardinal Wolsey's household and a regular at court, he made it his habit to drift by the queen's lodgings, to dally with the ladies, and there the harebrained Henry fell for the siren Anne Boleyn. He had been long promised by his father to Mary Talbot, daughter of the Earl of Shrewsbury, but while these two nobles hammered out the terms of the dynastic match, Percy and Anne were secretly betrothed. Unfortunately for him, he faced competition from an indomitable adversary. The king having confided to Wolsey his passion for the same bewitching young woman, Wolsey excoriated the weeping youth, in front of servants, at York Place, his palace at Whitehall. "I marvel not a little of thy peevish folly that thou wouldst tangle and ensure thyself with a foolish girl yonder in the court… Dost thou not consider the estate that God hath called thee unto in this world?"

The Earl was alerted and came thundering down from the North to denounce his "proud, presumptuous, disdainful and very unthrifty waster" of a son. The union of Anne and Henry Percy was never to be allowed, and Wolsey was never to be forgiven. Anne was sent from court to cool her heels at Hever, vowing that if ever it lay in her power to do the cardinal harm, she would do so—"as she did indeed, after," recorded George Cavendish, Wolsey's Gentleman Usher and posthumous biographer. As she did indeed.

✨ The perfect courtier without flaw

Urbino, Italy, 1508. Count Baldassare Castiglione sits down to pen a witty, erudite work that will become an international bestseller. Chuckling, frowning, raising his eyebrows, he will in a few days have prepared a first draft. But he will not be satisfied with it, and his work will be several years in the writing…

The Book of the Courtier was finally published in 1528, to be devoured by the *haut monde* of France, Italy, Spain, Germany, the Netherlands, and Poland.

BELOW: *Renaissance man Baldassare Castiglione, soldier, diplomat, aristocrat at the court of Urbino, by his friend Raphael. His* Book of the Courtier *set out to define the qualities of the ideal courtier. It became an international bestseller and had a profound influence upon Henry's court.*

Castiglione was an aristocrat, a diplomat, a friend of the painter Raphael, and a cavalier at the ducal palazzo of Guidobaldo da Montefeltro. The Urbino court was the acme of culture and refinement, famed for its music, plays, and poetry recitals, organized by Elisabetta, Duchess of Urbino. From his seminal tome we see that, in the courts of Renaissance princes, fashion went far beyond clothing. The modish courtier was expected to have many accomplishments, to conform to exacting standards of decorum, to indulge in displays of chivalric romance, and to manifest "beautiful behavior."

Set over the course of four nights, Castiglione's book takes the form of discussions, with various protagonists giving voice to their perceptions, as the Duchess steers the conversation. The author's task was to describe the "form of Courtiership most befitting a gentleman who lives at the court of princes, by which he may have the ability and knowledge perfectly to serve them… in short, what manner of man he ought to be who may deserve to be called a perfect Courtier without flaw."

This paragon was to be endowed by nature with beauty of countenance and person, the ability to read music and to play various instruments, and the skill of horseman and hunter "because the chase bears a certain likeness to war: and truly it is an amusement for great lords." Tennis was deemed an admirable exercise, to show "the disposition of the body, the quickness and suppleness of every member." Literacy, Greek, Latin, the humanities were prerequisites, as was "a good voice... sonorous and clear, sweet and well sounding."

Self-aggrandizement, braggadocio, presumption, tattling, flattery, foul language, and indecency were frowned upon, along with such infantile pranks as startling horses, pushing one another downstairs, and, at table, throwing soups, sauces, and jellies.

Women did not escape the scrutiny of Castiglione, who lauded those who used makeup subtly:

Do you not see how much more grace a lady has who paints (if at all) so sparingly and so little, that whoever sees her is in doubt whether she be painted or not; than another lady so plastered that she seems to have put a mask upon her face and dares not laugh for fear of cracking it...? Again, how much more pleasing than all others is one... who is plainly seen to have nothing on her face, although to be neither very white nor very red, but by nature a little pale and sometimes tinged with an honest flush from shame or other accident...

Tennis, hunting, music, games, jest... Castiglione could have been describing the court of Henry VIII, where Anne Boleyn, so subtle in her makeup, neither very white nor very red, and so adroit in conversation, arrived like the cat among the pigeons. She played the lute, harp, and virginal and sang sweetly. She excelled at the game of courtly love, an elaborate, mannered ritual of flirtation entailing gentle banter, punning, fortune-telling, riddles, verse, serenades, and words and deeds of gallantry—none of which was in Katharine's staid repertoire.

🕊 Bards of passion and of mirth

Castiglione's model courtier was to be "well versed in the poets... and also proficient in writing verse and prose... for besides the enjoyment he will find in it, he will by this means never lack agreeable entertainment with ladies, who are usually fond of such things."

OPPOSITE: *The feminine arts were highly prized at court. These three women are making chamber music with the voice, a lute, and a flute, so popular in the Renaissance. They wear the French hoods for which Anne Boleyn set the style. Anne was accomplished at music and dance and played the virginal and the lute. At least two verses are attributed to her, including "Defiled is My Name Full Sore"—as defiled it would be.*

Greate and Costly Array and Apparrell **67**

OPPOSITE: *Holbein's sketch of Henry Howard, Earl of Surrey, first son of Thomas Howard, 3rd Duke of Norfolk. A soldier poet, with his friend Thomas Wyatt he introduced the sonnet form to English verse. He was a cousin of Kathryn Howard, Henry's fifth wife. Rash and reckless, Howard was once imprisoned for breaking the windows of sleeping Londoners, justifying his actions in* A Satire against the Citizens of London.

Poetry flourished under Henry, where patronage was a mixed blessing, as writing that praised the mighty monarch was inevitably favored over anything that smacked of dissent. Toadyism did not, however, entirely triumph over talent. Some remarkably beautiful verse was produced within an atmosphere of tyranny and suppression.

Among the courtier poets were Anne's brother, George Boleyn, and Henry Howard, Earl of Surrey. Boleyn's work has not survived, unless in one poem that is perhaps by him, *The Lover Complaineth the Unkindess of His Love* and/or in *Oh Death, Rock Me Asleep*, alternatively attributed to Anne. (Death would rock the Boleyn siblings to sleep in 1536 and the sonneteer Earl of Surrey in 1547, at Henry's behest, but that is still in the future.)

John Skelton, Henry's old tutor in the service of Henry VII, having taken himself off to become a deacon, produced *The Bowge of Court,* a satire on the vice, duplicity and dangers of court life. He relinquished the rectorship of Diss, Norfolk, in 1512 to return to Henry VIII's court, but then, in the early 1520s, when he was in his 60s, from his retirement quarters in the precincts of Westminster Abbey he began firing off vicious satires such as *Colin Clout,* lampooning Henry's favorite cardinal, Thomas Wolsey, in the style of a 16th-century Eminem.

Say this, and say that,
His head is so fat,
He wotteth never what
Nor wherefore of he speaketh;
He crieth and he creaketh,
He prieth and he peaketh,
He chides and he chatters,
He prates and he patters,
He clitters and he clatters,
He meddles and he smatters,
He gloses and he flatters…

Did Skelton have a death wish? How dared he turn out such scurrilous polemic? While he named no name, he eschewed the veiled language employed by men such as the gentleman poet Sir Thomas Wyatt, known, with Henry Howard, as a "Father of the English Sonnet." A dashing figure who found himself desperately attracted to Anne, Wyatt was, however, married, although separated; she could not aspire to be his wife. We may suspect a cruel streak in the way she teased and tantalized him—but, then, this was the way of courtly love. Later Wyatt would spend time in the Tower accused of adultery with Anne. His life was spared, and he was freed, but a poem expressing his despair at loss of her to the king stands as an affecting testament to his regret.

ABOVE: *Henry VIII was himself a lyricist. This walnut and oak writing box may have been his. It is adorned with the badges of Henry and Katharine of Aragon and with mythological figures.*

OPPOSITE: *"The Bell Tower showed me such sight/That in my head sticks day and night." Another pioneer of the English sonnet form, Sir Thomas Wyatt, shown here in a copy of a sketch by Holbein, was smitten by Anne Boleyn—and had the horror of seeing her beheaded while he was imprisoned in the Bell Tower of the Tower of London.*

Whoso list to hunt

Whoso list to hunt, I know where is an hind,
But as for me, alas, I may no more;
The vain travail hath wearied me so sore,
I am of them that furthest come behind.
Yet may I by no means my wearied mind
Draw from the deer, but as she fleeth afore
Fainting I follow; I leave off therefore,
Since in a net I seek to hold the wind.
Who list her hunt, I put him out of doubt,
As well as I, may spend his time in vain.
And graven with diamonds in letters plain,
There is written her fair neck round about,
"Noli me tangere, for Caesar's I am,
And wild for to hold, though I seem tame."

"*Noli me tangere:* Touch me not," is from the Bible, John 20:17. Henry, too, at this time, has been reading his Bible, mining it for gems, such as Leviticus 20:21: "And if a man shall take his brother's wife, it is an unclean thing: he hath uncovered his brother's nakedness, they shall be childless." In marrying Katharine he had transgressed God's law. *This* is why he was denied a son. This is why he must be free to marry Anne.

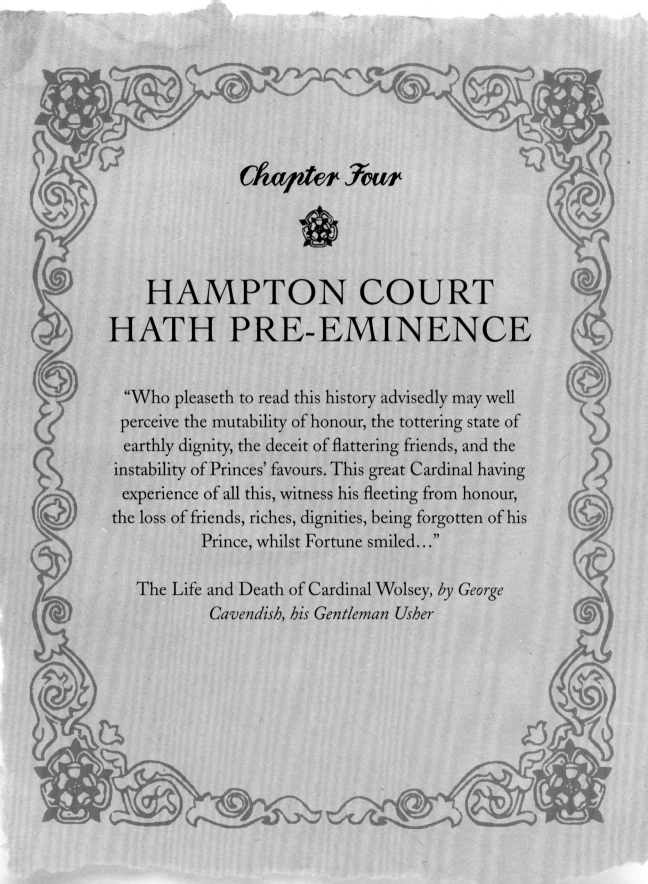

Chapter Four

HAMPTON COURT HATH PRE-EMINENCE

"Who pleaseth to read this history advisedly may well perceive the mutability of honour, the tottering state of earthly dignity, the deceit of flattering friends, and the instability of Princes' favours. This great Cardinal having experience of all this, witness his fleeting from honour, the loss of friends, riches, dignities, being forgotten of his Prince, whilst Fortune smiled…"

The Life and Death of Cardinal Wolsey, *by George Cavendish, his Gentleman Usher*

Cardinal Wolsey sits to dine, a study in scarlet, on a Chair of Estate fringed with Venetian gold, beneath a golden Canopy of Estate. He is not a well man. Repeated bouts of the sweating sickness, stones, quinsy, dropsy, colic, and ague have played havoc with his digestion. The physicians from London and Padua who advised him to build his redbrick Renaissance palace at Hampton, within a loop of the Thames, extolled the "extraordinary salubrity" of the site.

---

*W*olsey is more than ten miles as the crow flies, some twenty by barge up the snaking river, from the stench and stews, the fires and filth, the rats, bawds, and beggars of the capital. He has fresh air and piped springwater, but he is ailing nonetheless. He can take only soft food, and has dispensation from the Pope to eat meat in Lententide. "Capons stewed, fesaunt and partriche mewed… pigges in Lent… all manner of fleesh meat…" When he recalls the jibes of that scoundrel poet John Skelton, the repast turns to chaff in his mouth.

Well, let such men mock! Things could be worse. He is still the king's First Minister, his "awne goode cardinal." Henry may not clap an arm about his shoulder and walk with him in gardens, as of old, but he sends him pills and exhorts him to take fresh air and exercise. For the son of an Ipswich "kill-cow", the cardinal has done all right.

Some 500 retainers answer to him. Visitors must walk through eight rooms to reach him in his audience chamber. His banquets and his entertainments are legendary. Not Cleopatra, nor Caligula, ever laid on such feasts, the Venetian ambassador has reported. At Hampton Court there are beds for 280 guests, hundreds with feather mattresses, with posts of carved oak, drapes and canopies of satin and velvet, and counterpanes of embroidered damask. The four gilded posts of His Eminence's "Great Riche Bedstede" are topped with carved boules and cardinal's hats. His trussing bed, which can be taken apart, packed up and transported with him wherever he goes, is made of alabaster and decorated with his coat of arms, depicted in flowers and gilt on the sides.

He has 600 tapestries, which he changes around weekly. Some are from his bishoprics, others specially commissioned, wrought by teams of Flemish weavers and two years in the making. Biblical scenes abound—the stories of Moses, King David, St John the Baptist, St George, Christ casting the money changers from the temple, Samson beguiled by Delilah. Everywhere, too, the

eye is diverted by allegory and scenes from mythology—here it falls upon Paris and Achilles, there it encounters Hannibal, The Wheel of Fortune, and The Pilgrimage of the Life of Man. Wavering torchlight animates plump cherubs, Dame Pleasaunce, Pluto and Ceres, and "The Duke of Bry and the Giant Orrible." The Nine Worthies preside in the Great Chamber. The Seven Deadly Sins look down on Wolsey as he composes himself for sleep. "Hangings of verdures" portray the natural world, flora and fauna, men shooting, hawking, woodcutting, "a man kneeling on his hat, and putting a duck's bill in the ground…"

The Tuscan sculptors Giovanni da Maiano (who crafted the medallions at Hampton Court Palace) and Benedetto da Rovezzano have begun work on a black marble sarcophagus for Wolsey's solemn burial, already planned for the grounds at Windsor. Started in 1524, and not yet complete, the tomb will be a fine and fitting memorial to the Cardinal when he is carried by angels to Abraham's bosom (but, pray, let that not be yet!).

Wolsey's stores of silver and gold—sideboards and cupboards groaning with goblets, flagons, ewers, plates and dishes, antique and "of the most newest fashions," studded with diamonds and rubies—are beyond price.

OPPOSITE: *The great glory of the Chapel Royal, Hampton Court, is the ceiling of "byse" blue and gold, commissioned by Henry from 1535 and built of oaks from Windsor Forest. The king's arms, the Tudor rose, and heraldic badges ornament the tops of the walls. It was in the Chapel, in 1541, that Archbishop Thomas Cranmer handed Henry a letter that would shatter his illusions about his fifth wife, Kathryn Howard (see page 157).*

For his Gentleman Usher George Cavendish, the Chapel, with its "costly ornaments and rich jewells", copes and candlesticks, crosses, censers and chalices, beggars description.

John Skelton has derided Wolsey in his poems *Colin Clout* and *Speke, Parrot*. In his most devastating piece, however, there can be no mistaking the message:

Why come ye not to court?
To which court?
To the King's court,
Or to Hampton Court?
Nay, to the King's court!
The King's court
Should have excellence
But Hampton Court
Hath the pre-eminence…

Cardinal Wolsey has forgotten what it means to be a Christian—to live in the way of Christ. He has forgotten the vows of celibacy, with a baseborn son and daughter grown to adulthood. He has forgotten any notion of humility. He has forgotten that his god is a jealous god. This much, though, he cannot forget: his king is a jealous king.

Wolsey the prideful

In the good times—and there were *such* good times—Henry delighted to visit Wolsey at Hampton Court. In March 1514 he brought Katharine to view the old manor that his cardinal had acquired with plans to rebuild to a fabulously up-to-the-minute design. By May 1516 the construction of the new palace was sufficiently well in hand and the interiors opulent enough to receive Henry and Katharine to dine.

The cardinal's palace was always at the king's disposal. As well as Wolsey's own private chambers there were apartments for Henry, Katharine, and Princess Mary. Wolsey's biographer George Cavendish recalls:

When it pleased the king's majesty for his recreation, to repair unto the cardinal's house, as he did divers times in the year… there wanted no preparation, or goodly furniture, with viands of the finest sort, that

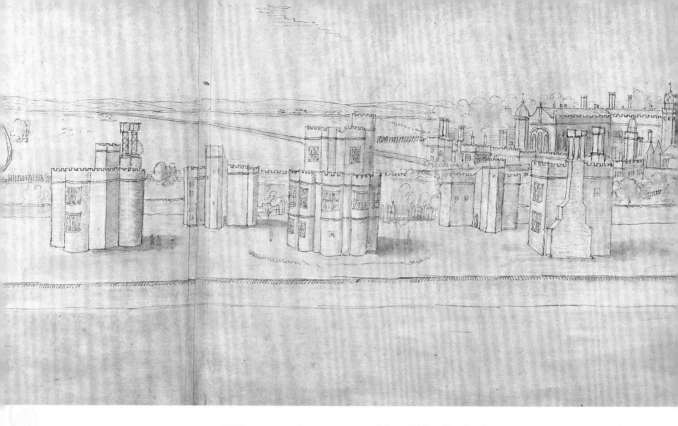

could be gotten for money or friendship. Such pleasures were then devised for the king's comfort and consolation, as might be invented or by man's wit imagined. Banquets were set forth, masques and mummeries in so gorgeous a sort, and costly manner, that it was heaven to behold.

Certainly Wolsey gloated over his status and possessions. Certainly he was no stranger to his mirror. On becoming a cardinal in 1515, he at once wrote off to Rome for "two or three hoods of such patterns and colours as Cardinals be wont to wear there… with two great pieces of silk used by Cardinals there for making the kirtles and other like garments."

He granted audiences while seated on a gold throne, resplendent in robes of crimson or scarlet satin, taffeta, or damask. Upon his head he wore "a round pillion with a neck of black velvet," and about his neck a tippet of sable.

Yet in one sense all this was his homage to Henry. He had to manifest the quality of magnificence befitting the king's First Minister. In his own words, he represented "the king's majesty's person in all the high courts of this realm, to the terror and keeping down of all rebellious treasons, traitors, all the wicked and corrupt members of this commonwealth." Visiting ambassadors, reeling from the splendor, would "make a glorious report in their country, to the King's honour and that of his realm."

At the very least, Hampton Court was the ultimate prodigy house, built with no higher purpose than to accommodate and entertain the sovereign and his entourage; at most, it was always Henry's own. Wolsey fudged the issue. When writing to the king he signed off with "From your Grace's manor at Hampton Court"—although in other correspondence it would be "From my manor at Hampton Court." At some date around the summer of 1525, the issue was resolved, when Henry testily demanded to know why the cardinal had built so splendiferous a mansion for himself. "To show how noble a place a subject may offer his sovereign," came the quick reply, at which Henry took immediate ownership of palace and contents. Some ambiguity remained, as Wolsey continued to use Hampton Court as he had always done, but the grand gesture was received without a thank you, and failed to boost the cardinal's diminished standing with the covetous monarch.

Four years later, in 1529, the king would show his gratitude by adding the cardinal's London residence, York Place, to his property portfolio, as Wolsey's world unraveled.

Even those who hold no brief for Cardinal Wolsey would see that he was ill-used. Some 16 years Henry's senior, he had been stalwart, indefatigable, and indispensable. He was politically astute, with both winning affability and rat-like cunning. In person he could be brusque, aloof, abrupt, imperious, making people wait in vain to meet with him. He would hold to his nose the peel of an orange filled with sponge soaked in vinegar and "other confections against the pestilent airs"—although this, given his precarious health and the prevalence of plague, can be understood. He was a man of contradictions, "lofty and sour" to those who opposed him, "sweet as summer" to his friends.

Henry had delegated almost entire control of foreign policy to Wolsey. It was Wolsey who masterminded a successful campaign against the French in 1513 and negotiated peace in 1514, when Henry's little sister, Mary Tudor, aged 18, was married off to the 52-year-old Louis XII. In 1520, the Field of Cloth of Gold had been a triumph of Wolsey's organizational skills. He oversaw all the correspondence of state. By his international maneuvering he had raised England "from a third-rate state of little account into the highest circle of European politics." His gray hair he attributed to serving Henry more diligently than he had served God. But, when it came to the king's "Great Matter," the annulment of his marriage to Katharine so that he might marry Anne, Wolsey was not to prevail. "If the Pope is not compliant, my own life will be shortened," he wrote prophetically. The Pope was not compliant.

How are the mighty fallen

My Lord, though you are a man of great understanding, you cannot avoid being censured by everybody for having drawn on yourself the hatred of a king who had raised you to the highest degree to which the greatest ambition of a man seeking his fortune can aspire. I cannot comprehend, and the king still less, how your reverent lordship, after having allured us by many fine promises about divorce, can have repented of your purpose, and how you could have done what you have, in order to hinder the consummation of it… But, for the future, I shall rely on nothing but the protection of Heaven and the love of my dear king, which alone will be able to set right again those plans which you have broken and spoiled…

BELOW: *This portrait, above all, is how we picture Anne Boleyn—but is it Anne? Not content with wiping her off the face of the earth, Henry sought to destroy every image of her. What we see today are later copies of lost works. Some people question why the subject wears a "B" pendant, not Anne's preferred "A."*

Here was Anne Boleyn, spitting tacks, in a letter to Thomas Wolsey in October 1529. If the tone finds a queasy response in the reader today, it must have shaken the already fragile, desperate cardinal to the core.

Anne and Henry were by this time convinced—if we believe Cavendish, *she* had convinced Henry—that Wolsey had been working against them, secretly supporting Katharine, to ensure that Anne would never be queen.

On July 5, 1529, Wolsey had quit Hampton Court for what was to be the last time, to attend a hearing at London's Blackfriars. It was a rotten summer—had been, indeed, a rotten two years. In the winter of 1526–7, downpours had "destroyed cornfields, pastures and beasts," and there was worse to come. On April 2 the heavens opened, and the rain did not stop until June 3.

In late May 1528, an outbreak of sweating sickness in London had become an epidemic, spreading to the north of England. Anne Boleyn was one of those who fell ill—and pulled through. Henry had broken up his court and retreated from London, moving between palaces, and though he

failed to rush to her side, he had dictated a letter, assuring her that he desired her health as his own, "so that I would gladly bear half your illness to make you well." He sent his second favorite physician, the top man being absent, begging her to follow his advice.

It was against this background of crop failures, starvation, food riots, and deadly disease that Henry continued to press ahead with his remorseless campaign to have his marriage annulled. His case rested upon the convenient religious conviction, derived from Leviticus, that in marrying his brother's widow he had unwittingly broken God's law.

Yes, he had a daughter whom he loved with all his twisted heart. He and Katharine were entranced with their princess and much involved in her upbringing. Aged nine, as Henry's sole heir, Mary had been sent for a time to Ludlow Castle as *de facto* Princess of Wales. In the summer of 1529, she was 13, a petite girl like her mother, musical like her father, a good scholar, fluent in several languages. It was not to deny her existence that Henry resorted to the scriptures. He did, however, contrive a theory that the reference to "children" in Leviticus was a mistranslation; it should obviously have read "sons." Henry was nothing as straightforward as an outright liar; he just took inconvenient truths and tortured them into a shape to suit him.

Katharine was meanwhile contending that her marriage to Arthur had not been consummated—she would swear it under oath and never recant—so there was no sin in the eyes of God, in her marriage to Henry.

From May 1529, Thomas Wolsey and Lorenzo Campeggio, fellow cardinals and papal legates, had the onerous task of presiding over a tribunal at Blackfriars, to sift the arguments. Their interests, like those of Henry and Katharine, were diametrically opposed. Campeggio, in agony with gout and speaking scant English, needed to satisfy the papacy; Wolsey was desperate to please the king.

Katharine appeared once at the hearings, where she fell on her knees before Henry and implored him, for all the love that had been between them, to accord her justice and to show her compassion. As God was her witness, she put it to his conscience, "When ye had me at the first… I was a true maid, without the touch of man." She had, she was not slow to remind Henry, borne him several children, although it had pleased God to call them out of this world.

"Stubborn" is a word commonly used to describe Katharine of Aragon. Why could she not have retired to a nunnery to live the contemplative life, as had been asked of her? But then again, *why should she?* She valued her estate as wife queen, and, extraordinary as it may seem, she was, or professed to be, in love with her husband. Whatever drove her, she gave, that day, a bravura performance, then swept out, defying every summons to return. For this contempt she was judged contumacious, willfully defiant, but she did well to stay away.

Amid theological argument, testimony, claim and counterclaim, the whole unedifying debate turned on one question—had Arthur or had he not had carnal knowledge of his wife? It came down almost literally to airing dirty linen in public, when at one point Wolsey threatened to produce a report of bloodstained sheets, allegedly sent to her parents, Ferdinand and Isabella, as evidence of her loss of her virginity.

Henry, descending to pure cant, insisted that, not for "carnal concupiscence," nor for dislike of the queen's person or age, but for the good of the realm, he must take a young wife to bear him a male heir. If, however, it were found that his union could stand within God's law, he would be as content to continue in it with Katharine as with any woman alive.

On Friday, July 25, Campeggio made an announcement that would dash Anne's hopes for the summer wedding upon which she had set her heart. The proceedings were adjourned. Pope Clement VII had decreed that the case must transfer to Rome.

OPPOSITE: *William Hogarth's dramatic 1727 representation of "Henry VIII bringing to court Anne Bullen, who was afterwards his royal comfort… The daring Harry stands… with lovely Anne Bullen joining hands, her looks bespeaking ev'ry heav'nly grace." On the right of the engraving sits Wolsey beneath a canopy of estate, his looks bespeaking frustration and despair.*

In the long weeks of unbearable anxiety that followed, Wolsey was forced to endure the flatter–batter treatment from the vacillating king—now banished from the imagined Camelot, forbidden to step within three miles of court, now summoned to the presence and, to Anne's fury, closeted with the king.

George Cavendish had it from a servant who had waited on Henry and Anne at dinner in her chamber and heard her say to him:

Sir, is it not a marvel to think what debt and danger the cardinal hath brought you in with all your subjects? ...What things hath he wrought within this realm to your great slander and dishonour? ... If my lord of Norfolk, my lord of Suffolk, my lord my father, or any other noble person within your realm had done much less than he, but they should have lost their heads.

In other words: send the cardinal to the scaffold.

On October 9, 1529, Wolsey was charged under 14th-century law with praemunire, the crime of exercising papal power in England to the detriment of the king or his people. As papal legate he was a sitting duck. The prescribed punishment was imprisonment at the king's pleasure and confiscation of all his properties.

Henry spared Wolsey prison but banished him to his small palace at Esher, southwest of London, and snapped up York Place, in Whitehall. When Henry brought Anne from Greenwich to inspect her new London residence, she was full of glee, thrilled not just with the tapestries, gold plate, and fine furnishings but by the lack of any apartment for Queen Katharine. Adjacent houses could be demolished to create space for a garden, and this would be Henry's future town house, which became known as Whitehall Palace.

❧ His grace's own manor

Now Henry truly came into his own at Hampton Court. Katharine accompanied him there after the cardinal's banishment, where they acted toward one another with the utmost civility. Henry was inwardly seething, still hell-bent upon divorce, and the apartment into which Anne moved at the palace had been in preparation back in 1528. But he and Katharine *were* still king and queen, figureheads with ceremonial functions to perform. Their roles demanded that they be seen together, speak together, dine together. The conduct of the king and queen, their "reciprocal courtesy" and "utmost mental tranquility," struck the Milanese ambassador, Augustino Scarpinello, as "more than human."

Soon Henry's badge and coat of arms were carved into the building's fabric, as painters, carvers, bricklayers, masons, and joiners swarmed over it. All around, in wooded Surrey, trees were felled by the dozen for timber. There

ABOVE: *Henry VIII's plans for a bigger, better Hampton Court Palace included a new Great Hall large enough to accommodate his court for the great festivals of Christmas and Twelfth Night. Six of an ensemble of ten Brussels tapestries commissioned by Henry, depicting the biblical story of Abraham, hang here.*

were shipments of the beautiful pale Caen stone from northwest France. Pinnacles bristled with gilded heraldic beasts. Wolsey's Great Hall was demolished and a bigger, better "King's New Hall" went up, to be hung, on completion, with ten tapestries devoted to "The Story of Abraham." In the much-extended accommodation, there were a thousand hearths in which fires must be lit.

Henry built for his own use a new gallery, a library stocked with Wolsey's books from Whitehall, and a study in which to work on his writing. Henry's treatise *Defence of the Seven Sacraments*, a Catholic polemic against the religious reforms of Martin Luther, penned in 1519–21 and dedicated to Pope

Leo X, had earned him the accolade "Defender of the Faith" in 1521. Now he was busily engaged on *A Glasse of the Truthe*, a specious, self-serving tract in support of his divorce. It took the form of "a small dialogue between a lawyer and a divine," in which the divine came down squarely on Henry's side, quoting Leviticus, chapter and verse. "Who taught you, I pray you, to hit so truly the nail on the head?" the divine enquired of Henry's lawyer alter ego, before opining "verily there was never prince among us that was ever better beloved, nor that hath deserved more to be… Methinketh the king's highness and his parliament should earnestly press the metropolitans of this realm (their unjust oath to the pope notwithstanding) to set an end shortly in this." Deuteronomy's injunction that a man should marry his brother's widow was "truly to be observed in the mystical sense than the literal."

The Italian artist Antonio Toto del Nunziata was commissioned to paint religious pictures in Henry's library and closet. "The burying of Our Lord." "The burying of Our Blessed Lady." Adam delving in the ground. Adam, like poor old Wolsey, driven out of Paradise… "Antonye Tote," as he appears in the ledger, had been dispatched from Florence by the sculptor Pietro Torrigiano back in 1519 to work on a tomb for the king. This was never realized, but no matter, as it must have seemed to Henry, since he now owned Wolsey's black marble sarcophagus, only awaiting completion.

In ten years of expansion, Hampton Court was transformed into one of the most modern and sophisticated palaces in Henry's possession, with an enormous kitchen complex (described in Chapter Six). As well as his library and study, Henry's suite comprised a bedchamber, a strong room, and a new bathroom, equipped with copper baths. Pipes laid for Wolsey brought springwater from Coombe Hill in Kingston three miles away. The bath was fed, via taps for hot and cold, from cisterns on the floor above, where water was heated by a charcoal-fired stove.

For his intimate ablutions, he still had Henry Norris, his Groom of the Stool, at hand as he sat enthroned on his latrine clad in black velvet. The private "garderobes" of the most royal and noble members of the court were equipped with shafts to the moat. Less important householders had use of the new "Great House of Easement," or "common jakes," a two-story, 28-seater lavatory that disgorged effluent into the moat via brick-lined drains, to be carried away by the river. The sign of the cross was painted in dark corners of the palace where lazy souls were in the habit of urinating. Small boys known as "gong scourers" had the job of crawling into the drains to clean them.

Henry liked to be clean, but he would not come up smelling of roses.

ABOVE: *For his Renaissance-style palace, Henry naturally wanted a knot garden—so fashionable in Tudor times. Inspired by the gardens of Italy, they featured geometric plantings and intricate, interlacing designs that often played on symbolism and puzzles.*

❧ A garden of delights

No sooner had the king relieved Wolsey of his property and put in hand his improvements to the palace than he turned his attention to the pleasure gardens that Wolsey had begun in the Renaissance manner.

At Richmond, Henry VII had had "most fair and pleasant gardens, with royal knots alleyed and herbs... with many vines, seeds and strange fruit, right goodly beset," but with Henry VIII at Hampton Court the gardens became yet another emphatic assertion of royal prestige and power.

Wolsey's scheme included orchards and gardens with dividing walls of brick, as well as a park, with a surrounding moat. We have a charming evocation from George Cavendish:

My gardens sweet, enclosed with walles strong,
Embanked with benches to sytt and take my rest
The knotts so enknotted it cannot be exprest.
With arbours and alys so plesaunt and so dulce
The pestylent ayers with flavors to repulse.

Henry's larger vision included a Privy Garden between the palace and the Thames for his personal use and to make a stunning first impression on visitors arriving by water. A fashionable "mount," a vast earth mound, was raised and planted with trees. At the summit was a banqueting house (one of a number) glinting with glass, approached by a spiral path. The plans for the garden were influenced by the capricious English weather, with elegant garden houses and sheltered "galleries" or walkways for rainy days, and arbors, bowers, shady corners, and "roosting places" for hot summer days.

Everywhere there reared up "The King's Beasts" on posts striped with the Tudor colors of green and white, symbolizing eternity and purity. Carved from wood or stone, and bearing shields, were such mythical creatures as dragons, griffins, and unicorns, scarcely less fantastical lions, tigers, and leopards, and the more familiar greyhound, hart, and bull, brightly painted in heraldic sable, gules, azure, vert, silver, and gold. That peculiar Tudor favorite the knot garden was clearly a feature—elaborate patterns, perhaps raised, and surrounded by clipped box—as well as railed gardens, fountains, and topiary. As Henry looked to Italy for inspiration, sundials and statuary of Roman times made a reappearance.

Like the old monastery gardens, the palace gardens and park were not just a place of beauty and pleasure, but a living larder. Ponds were stocked with fish. Deer were on the hoof; hares on the hop. A rabbit warren was built. Plots were planted with culinary and medicinal herbs, which would have included, according to courtier Thomas Tusser's poem *Five Hundred Points of Good Husbandrie*, basil, chamomile, lemon balm, cowslips, fennel, germander, hyssop, lavender, marjoram, camphor, sage, savory, pennyroyal, tansy, and mint. The orchards provided abundant fruit. There are accounts of sums paid to gardeners for deliveries of damsons, pears, filberts, and the cherries of which the king was particularly fond, perhaps for their laxative effect since he was a martyr to constipation. An ornate drawbridge connected the Great Orchard and the King's Private Orchard, between which was a moat.

Flowers were not of the greatest importance in the palace gardens, although there were old-fashioned English favorites, such as roses, rosemary, gillyflowers, and violets.

Bowling alleys, tennis courts (open-air and "close"), an enormous tiltyard complete with viewing towers and the pavilions of the champions, as well as his beloved deer chase, provided diversions for the king. He thrilled to ride out with Anne, and to teach her to shoot at targets. He was at Hampton Court, enjoying a spot of archery, in November 1530, when dear George Cavendish arrived, deferential and shaken, bearing the news that Wolsey had died at Leicester Abbey on his journey from York to stand trial for treason. "Father," Wolsey had told the abbot, "I have come to lay my bones among you."

Wolsey was buried, not at Windsor as he had planned, but in the Lady Chapel at Leicester. No trace of his tomb has been found, and it is suggested that it may have been destroyed later in Henry's reign, though his black marble sarcophagus, on which Henry had designs, can be seen in the crypt at St Paul's Cathedral. It was still unfinished when its Italian sculptors quit England in the Reformation. So it was that, in January 1806, that great admiral, Lord Nelson, would be buried in this thirdhand stone coffin designed for a cardinal.

*

Gratified though he was to own Hampton Court, Henry did not forsake his other palaces. The summer of 1531 found him at Windsor, preparing to set off on a progress with Anne at his side. On July 14, without forewarning or

RIGHT: *A Tudor garden to commemorate Henry's accession to the throne, five centuries before, was created in 2009, in Hampton Court's Chapel Court. Among the plantings of herbs and flowers, two replica King's Beasts (carved and painted wooden heraldic animals on poles) rear up, painted in heraldic colors. The Panther is spotted with gules and azure (red and blue), and breathes flame. The Yale has the body of an antelope and the tail of a lion; its horns, hooves, tufts of hair, crown (around its neck), and chain are gilded.*

farewell, he concocted a cock-and-bull story about hunting at Woodstock and took leave of Katharine. She was never to set eyes on him again.

In August, as he prepared to return to Windsor after staying with William Sandys at the Vyne, he sent orders for Katharine to be removed to The More, another house that Wolsey had once owned, near Rickmansworth in Hertfordshire. Mary was to be sent to Richmond. Katharine would never see *her* again either.

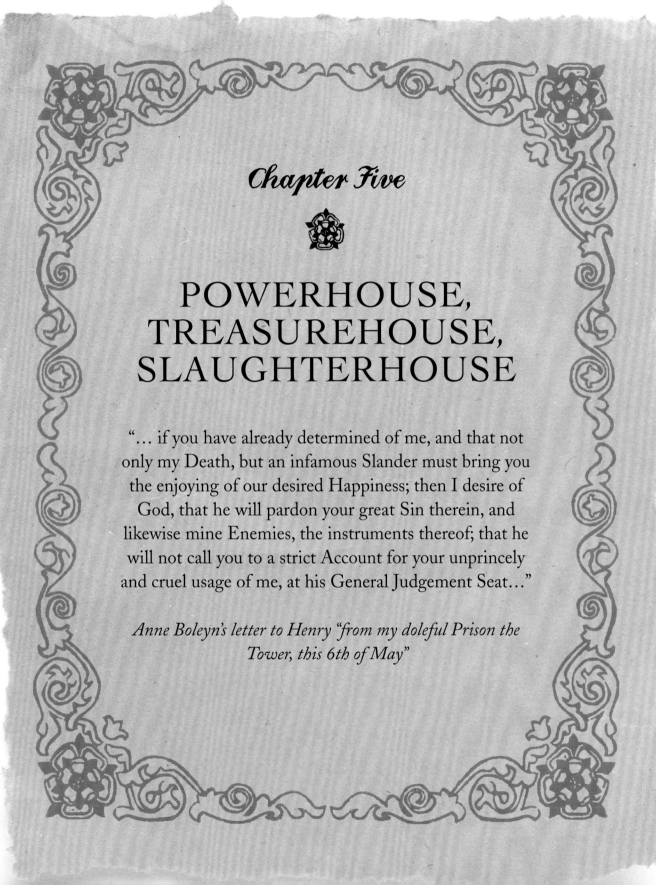

Chapter Five

POWERHOUSE, TREASUREHOUSE, SLAUGHTERHOUSE

"… if you have already determined of me, and that not only my Death, but an infamous Slander must bring you the enjoying of our desired Happiness; then I desire of God, that he will pardon your great Sin therein, and likewise mine Enemies, the instruments thereof; that he will not call you to a strict Account for your unprincely and cruel usage of me, at his General Judgement Seat…"

Anne Boleyn's letter to Henry "from my doleful Prison the Tower, this 6th of May"

On May 29, 1533, the Tower of London became the centerpiece for the celebrations of Anne Boleyn's day of days. The previous September Henry had created her Lady Marquess of Pembroke, and on or around January 25 he had entered into a form of marriage with her, in secret and somewhat in haste, for she was pregnant.

BELOW: *Anne's and Henry's entwined initials attest to the bond forged between them. When their marriage ended in travesty and tragedy, Henry sought to destroy the symbols of their love, but the sharp-eyed will spot survivors, such as this detail from a gate at Hampton Court.*

On May 23, Thomas Cranmer, Archbishop of Canterbury, had declared Henry's first marriage null and void, so that there might be no question of bigamy, thereby removing the last obstacle to Anne's elevation to queen.

Henry had been spending heavily on the Tower. Nearly £3,600 was sunk into refitting royal apartments, which ran between the Wardrobe Tower and Lanthorn (Lantern) Tower, with its Long Gallery, library, and garden. Some

3,000 tons of Caen stone were imported. The inner and outer curtain walls and White Tower were renovated, and the king's Master Carpenter, James Nedeham, was engaged to build a strong new timber roof for St Thomas's Tower, on the riverward side, to support cannons, to ensure that proceedings went with a bang.

Wynkyn de Worde, an Alsace-born London printer, was quick to capitalize on the historic event, with a full-color souvenir booklet, *The Noble Tryumphaunt Coronacyon of Quene Anne—Wyfe unto the Most Noble Kynge Henry VIII*. It tells how, as Anne waited at Greenwich, all the London guilds in their liveries—the Worshipful Companies of Fishmongers and Ironmongers, Brewers, Poulters, Saddlers, Coopers, Cutlers, Cordwainers—sailed in 50 barges downriver, with minstrels making sweet harmony and banners flying, all "comely beseen." At three o'clock, Anne stepped aboard a barge decked with innumerable pennants and draped with cloth of gold, for the short trip back upriver. She arrived at the Tower, where was fired more ordnance than any man could remember, and was received by the king with a noble, loving countenance. Crowds thronged both banks of the Thames, "wherein her grace with all her ladies rejoiced much."

De Worde prudently made no mention of the booing and cat-calling as Henry publicly kissed the bride so detested by his subjects. The couple spent the next two nights at the Tower, before Anne processed to Westminster Abbey under a canopy of gold. Her pregnancy concealed by extra panels of fabric, she was garbed in a kirtle of crimson velvet with ermine trim, and a purple velvet robe. Upon her head she wore a coronet with a cap of pearls and precious gems—at her throat, more pearls, huge and lustrous. Archly, she had chosen the motto "*La Plus Heureuse*" (The Most Happy), in contrast to Katharine's dull "Humble and Loyal."

Not four months later, on the afternoon of September 7, 1533, the new queen gave birth to a healthy baby. The girl, Elizabeth, who had been named after Henry's mother and who was born under Virgo, would live to be "the Virgin Queen," one of the greatest sovereigns in English history. But she was not a boy. Cancel the joust!

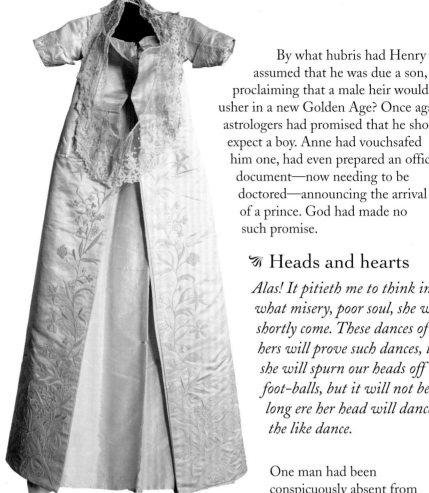

By what hubris had Henry assumed that he was due a son, proclaiming that a male heir would usher in a new Golden Age? Once again astrologers had promised that he should expect a boy. Anne had vouchsafed him one, had even prepared an official document—now needing to be doctored—announcing the arrival of a prince. God had made no such promise.

☙ Heads and hearts

Alas! It pitieth me to think into what misery, poor soul, she will shortly come. These dances of hers will prove such dances, that she will spurn our heads off like foot-balls, but it will not be long ere her head will dance the like dance.

RIGHT: *The christening gown worn by Princess Elizabeth for her baptism at Greenwich on September 10, 1533. Although disappointed of a boy child, Henry made a great occasion of the ceremony, with lords and ladies in attendance and a silver font.*

One man had been conspicuously absent from Anne's coronation. Though he had been sent £20 to buy robes for the occasion, Sir Thomas More had elected not to attend. A letter wishing Henry happiness and his bride good health took none of the sting out of the insult.

More had succeeded Wolsey as Lord Chancellor in 1529, but on May 16, 1532, the day after Henry effectively declared himself head of the Church, More had returned the Great Seal of England to the king and resigned.

Standing on his principles, he had refused to uphold the annulment of Henry's first marriage, or to support the Act of Succession by which Anne became queen and her offspring legal heirs to the throne. Nothing, now, would persuade him to endorse the Act of Supremacy, devised by Thomas Cromwell, asserting Henry as Supreme Head of the Church of England. "Maliciously, traitorously, diabolically," Sir Thomas More was defying his

Tho: Moor Ld Chancelour

sovereign. The Treasons Act 1534 was crafted to indict him, since, in February 1535, it became a capital crime to deprive "the king's most royal person, the queen's, or their heirs apparent… of their dignity, title, or name of their royal estates."

In the spring of 1535, as he passed his time in the Tower writing in charcoal *A Dialogue of Comfort against Tribulation* and preparing to meet his Maker, More received a visit from his eldest daughter, Meg Roper. By than, he had been a prisoner for almost a year, and was underfed and bodily weak, though as strong of mind as ever. Perhaps he felt a pang of yearning for the life on which he had turned his back, for he asked Meg how things were at court. Upon being told that for Anne Boleyn it was one round of dancing and sport, he predicted with eerie prescience how the queen's head would ere long "dance."

Sir Thomas's prison was the 12th-century Bell Tower, its Sussex marble footings lapped by the sludgy wash of the Thames. Above him, in the Upper Bell Tower, John Fisher, Bishop of Rochester, likewise awaited a martyr's death. Over their heads, in the wooden turret, at evening the curfew tolled the knell of passing day.

To More's wife, Alice, he was "playing the fool," preferring to "fondly tarry" in filth, among rats and mice, than to return to the bosom of the family at his "right fair" house in Chelsea, with his library, his gallery, his orchard and garden. He had only to swear allegiance to the king and he would have his liberty. "Tilly-vally!" Alice snorted at his response that the Tower was as close to Heaven as his own home.

It is hard to imagine that More was sincere in his expression of pity for Anne Boleyn. She was inimical to all that he held dear. At the time when William Tyndale's English-language Bible was being incinerated on the streets, she had been posturing at court with the Epistles of St Paul in French translation, playing Rose Red to Katharine's Snow White, in her quest for "the true path."

In May the new pope, Paul III, created the imprisoned John Fisher a cardinal, whereat an apoplectic Henry bellowed that he would "give him another hat, and send his head to receive his cardinal's hat afterwards." On June 22, Bishop Fisher was awakened at dawn to be told that he would that forenoon be getting that other hat. Henry sent word that he should make no emotive speech upon the scaffold and should avoid anything "touching his Majesty, whereby the people should have any cause to think of him, or his proceedings, otherwise than well."

That night found Henry attending a farce in which he was portrayed lopping off the heads of the clergy—such a rollicking good show that he ordered it to be repeated days later, for Anne's mirth.

Two weeks later, at 9 a.m. on July 6, a wan, bearded, emaciated More went to the scaffold, proclaiming himself "the king's good servant, but God's first." His spurned-off head was mounted on a pole on London Bridge, where it remained for some months, until Meg bought it for a relic before it could be tossed into the river.

Henry was at Windsor playing Tables with Anne when news reached him that More's execution was accomplished. According to Sir Thomas's great-grandson and biographer Cresacre More, the king glowered at Anne, terrible-eyed, and snarled, "You are the cause of this man's death!" Slapping

OPPOSITE: *The Bell Tower, begun in the reign of Richard the Lionheart and completed in the reign of the hapless King John, is the second-oldest tower in the fortress complex, after the White Tower. Sir Thomas More, who was at first held here in relative comfort and permitted visitors, had his creature comforts withdrawn one by one.*

down his cards, he stalked off to his chamber and sunk into melancholia, before sufficiently rallying to order the confiscation of More's right-fair house, and heading off on his summer progress.

Sir Thomas More had been zealous in pursuing "the king's gracious purpose" by battling the contagion of Lutheran heresy—for was not Henry styled Defender of the Faith? The Reformation that was to rip the Christian Church asunder had been creeping into England by the back door, despite the efforts of men such as More to barricade it. Then Henry himself threw the front door wide.

❧ La Plus Heureuse

With his divorce machinations, Henry VIII had torn Europe apart and set all Heaven in a rage, not for some deeply held religious principle, but to be free of Katharine and to marry Anne. It was to be a short marriage, but not a sweet one. For a powerful sense of how corrosive it became, we are indebted to one man.

Eustace Chapuys had arrived at court in September 1529. He was an ambassador of the Holy Roman Emperor, Katharine's nephew Charles V, and his sympathies were, of course, with Queen Katharine. But more than that, Anne Boleyn inspired in him such a visceral loathing that he could not write her name—she was, to him, "the Concubine," "the Whore"; Elizabeth was "the Bastard."

He was not, then, an unbiased observer, yet he was a lively commentator upon the fiasco of Henry's divorce and remarriage, and was not even above tipping his hat in grudging admiration to the "the King's mistress."

Having deserted Katharine at Windsor, Henry had returned her to the conditions from which he had rescued her more than 20 years before. After banishing her to The More in Hertfordshire, he had sent her to Ampthill in Bedfordshire, and by 1534 she was living out her days at Kimbolton Castle, Huntingdonshire, forbidden any contact with her daughter, unhappy girl, Henry's "pearl," who was being horrifyingly menaced and bullied.

"The Princess has been informed," wrote Chapuys, "that, by virtue of the statute lately passed… she must renounce her title… and that on pain of her life she must not call herself Princess or her mother Queen, but that if she ever does she will be sent to the Tower."

He was dismayed by the plight of Katharine, who was always, for him, "the Queen" (he disdained her new designation, "Dowager Princess of Wales"), as Mary was "the Princess." He repeatedly begged Thomas

RIGHT: *In this 16th-century portrait Anne wears a pendant with her initial and Henry's entwined. On the morning of her beheading she told Sir William Kingston, Constable of the Tower, "I heard say the executioner was very good, and I have a little neck," before putting her hands about it and laughing unnervingly.*

Cromwell to persuade Henry to reunite mother and daughter, or at least to restore some of Mary's old servants to her. He fretted that she was sick, that she needed better physicians, that her illness was caused by "distress and sorrow," and that someone might administer slow poison. He even went so far as to contemplate a rescue that would involve smuggling her aboard a ship for Spain.

The teenaged Mary was anathema to Anne. "She has boasted she will have the Princess for her lady's maid," Chapuys was reporting, even before Anne became queen. With the birth of Elizabeth, Anne had devised for Mary the humiliation of making her dance attendance on her half-sister. In December 1533 Mary had received a summons from Henry to attend court to serve the princess, to which she had responded icily that she knew of no other princess than herself.

Her admirable hauteur notwithstanding, when the infant Elizabeth was sent to Hatfield House in Hertfordshire (now Hatfield Old Palace), Mary was a member of her household. In a letter to Charles V, Chapuys wrote:

Last Thursday the Princess, who refused to accompany the Bastard on her removal to another house, was put by force by certain gentlemen into a litter… and thus compelled to make court to the said Bastard. She made a public protest of the compulsion used, and that her act should not prejudice her right and title. I should not have advised the Princess to have gone to this extreme, for fear of irritating her father, and consequently suffering worse treatment and some bad turn at the desire of his mistress, who is continually plotting the worst she can against the Princess.

Chapuys clearly saw the hand of Anne at work behind a puppet Henry, for "he dares neither say nor do except that which she commands him." An early hint that Henry was feeling hag-ridden also comes from Chapuys. Just before Anne retired to her chamber to await the birth of her baby, she had flown out at her husband for some kind of flirtation with a lady at court. "Shut your eyes," came the harsh reply, "and endure as your betters have done."

Anne had triumphed in subordinating Mary, she had robbed her of status and legitimacy, but she was by no means through. It gets worse, for why should the Treasons Act that had ensnared Sir Thomas More not apply also to Katharine and her daughter?

In February 1535, Chapuys received a letter from Katharine, through her physician, "stating that she was informed… that the King was determined again to attempt to make the Princess swear to the statutes passed against her mother and herself, and, on her refusal, would immediately put her to death, or at least to prison for life."

The ambassador was also, that month, to reveal details of another of Henry's dalliances. "The young lady who was lately in the King's favor is so no longer. There has succeeded to her place a cousin german [first cousin] of the concubine, daughter of the present *gouvernante* of the Princess." Anne Shelton, Mary's governess, was Thomas Boleyn's sister, and mother of daughters Margaret (Madge) and Mary (though some historians believe that Margaret and Mary were the same person). One or other was an attendant to Queen Anne and rumored to be Henry's mistress. Anne Boleyn was being paid in her own coin.

Anne meanwhile was calling upon her wiles to drive home her argument for the execution of Katharine and Mary. "The concubine has suborned a person to say that he has had a revelation from God that she cannot conceive while the said two ladies are alive," reported Chapuys in March 1535. He doubted not that she had spoken of it to the king and had sent the man to Cromwell. "She constantly speaks of them as rebels and traitresses deserving death."

By foul means or fouler, Mary feared, Anne would see her dead, as these excerpts from Chapuys's letters to Charles V reveal:

April 17: Ill as the Princess is, she does not cease to think if there be any means of escaping; and on this subject she had a long conversation with one of my men, begging me most urgently to think over the matter, otherwise she considered herself lost, knowing that they wanted only to kill her.

May 5: It is to be feared that if the King is getting so inured to cruelty he will use it towards the Queen and Princess, at least in secret; to which the concubine will urge him with all her power, who has lately several times blamed the said King, saying it was a shame to him and all the realm that they were not punished as traitresses according to the statutes. The said concubine is more haughty than ever, and ventures to tell the King that he is more bound to her than man can be to woman, for she extricated him from a state of sin; and moreover, that he came out of it the richest Prince that ever was in England, and that without her he would not have reformed the Church, to his own great profit and that of all the people.

July 25: The concubine… is incessantly crying after the King that he does not act with prudence in suffering the Queen and Princess to live, who deserved death more than those who have been executed, and that they were the cause of all.

Anne was furthermore trying to do down her own uncle. "I am informed on good authority that the said lady does not cease night or day to procure the disgrace of the Duke of Norfolk, whether it be because he has spoken too freely of her or because Cromwell, desiring to lower the great ones, wishes to commence with him."

ABOVE: *Charles V, Holy Roman Emperor from 1519 to 1556 (Charles I of Spain), was the nephew of Katharine of Aragon. He had just become king of Spain, at the age of 16, when this portrait was painted by Bernard van Orley. More for political than personal reasons, he supported his aunt's cause.*

OPPOSITE: *Thomas Howard, 3rd Duke of Norfolk, portrayed by Holbein. This great "noble" presided at the trial and execution of his niece Anne Boleyn, whose marriage to Henry he had naturally supported.*

The 3rd Duke of Norfolk, Thomas Howard, would complain that his niece treated him "worse than a dog." He was not alone among the lords at court in detesting Anne's arrogance. The valiant and once-loyal William Sandys feigned illness, retired to The Vyne, and took the risk of proposing to Chapuys that he let Charles V know that the people were so alienated by the king that he would find little resistance if he chose to "apply a remedy to the violence and disorder of England."

If Anne had lived to old age and not gone with such courage and dignity to her death, one wonders if she would have the cult following she has today.

✒ Final farewells

With failing strength and in unspeakable pain, at Kimbolton Castle, as her life slipped away, Katharine of Aragon dictated a gentle, reproving last letter to Henry. Defiant to the last, she signed it "Katharine the Quene":

My most dear lord, king and husband, The hour of my death now drawing on, the tender love I owe you forceth me, my case being such, to commend myself to you, and to put you in remembrance with a few words of the health and safeguard of your soul which you ought to prefer before all worldly matters, and before the care and pampering of your body, for the which you have cast me into many calamities and yourself into many troubles. For my part, I pardon you everything… Lastly, I make this vow, that mine eyes desire you above all things.

Chapuys had hastened to her bedside, and she drew comfort from his presence as they talked. On the afternoon of January 7, 1536—even then, to judge by her letter, loving Henry—Katharine died.

Within 24 hours the news had reached the king, and just as it is sometimes the fate of the messenger to be shot, so it may be his fortune to be rewarded. Anne's initial response to the tidings was to tip him handsomely.

Henry's reaction seems to have been one of relief, if we believe Chapuys. "God be praised that we are free from all suspicion of war!" he exclaimed, seeing how, now, he might mend relations with Charles V and thereby intimidate the French. Chapuys—who was no Sebastian Giustiniani in the art of the fashion note—recounted that "the following Sunday the King was clad all over in yellow, from top to toe, except the white feather he had in his bonnet, and the Little Bastard was conducted to Mass with trumpets and other great triumphs. After dinner the King… did several things like one transported with joy."

For all his malice toward Anne, Chapuys makes no mention of her dressing with similar irreverence, which casts doubts on accounts that she too wore yellow robes. Apart from anything else, it would not have suited her coloring, "sallow" as she was. As for Henry behaving "like one transported with joy," there were other reasons for elation. Anne was pregnant, sporting a "goodly belly." And besides, he was in love again.

With the elation around Katharine's death came responsibilities. Getting down to business, Henry engaged his Vice-Chamberlain, Sir Edward Baynton, to make an inventory of the late queen's robes and furs. Baynton sifted through Katharine's possessions and delivered to Henry some of the more desirable items. It is pitiful to note that during all these years she had kept a layette for some never-to-be child. And it makes one cringe to learn that tiny smocks and double petticoats, and a gold-fringed cloth to cover an infant, were "Delivered to the Queen."

When he rusticated Katharine, Henry had all but buried her. Now came the time to dispose of her mortal remains. A state funeral and interment with Prince Arthur at St Paul's would have been too emotive and extravagant, so she was taken to the very lovely Peterborough Cathedral, where her tomb today rates fourth on Visit England's list of the cathedral's attractions.

The funeral was held on January 29; on or close to that date, Anne Boleyn suffered what was probably at least her second miscarriage. The baby was "a man child."

It was becoming plain to Henry that, yet again, God was not to grant him a son. More and more he saw the reason for this, for Anne had used the black arts to cast a spell on him to make him marry her. Chapuys, meanwhile, with his ear to the ground as ever, had heard that the king had been making gifts to one "Miss Seymour," Jane, another of the queen's attendants. He clearly perceived the advantage to Henry of making another marriage—one that, in all eyes, would be lawful, and with a fertile younger woman.

Anne Boleyn had pressed, nagged, scolded, and schemed to see Katharine of Aragon dead, yet while Katharine lived Anne had been safe. Henry could not have borne the humiliation of admitting his mistake, or the pressure to return to his first queen.

We shall say goodbye to Anne without witnessing her fall or attending her trial, since after May 2 she was not to be again "at home with Henry." She was arrested at Greenwich and made the same journey by river as she had made three years before, to the Tower of London. She was accused of adultery,

incest, necromancy, and plotting Henry's murder. Her escort on the day was William Sandys, and her judge was her uncle Thomas Howard, 3rd Duke of Norfolk.

With her to their deaths were to go Anne's own brother George, accused of incest with her, and Sir Henry Norris, the handsome young musician Mark Smeaton (first tortured on the rack), Sir Francis Weston, and William Brereton, all accused of treason and adultery with Anne. All had been Henry's intimates, members of his Privy Chamber; Norris had been closer than any as his Groom of the Stool. None had a prayer of a fair trial.

On the sunny morning of May 19, 1536, Anne Boleyn was to make her ultimate fashion statement. Assured of her place in history and in Heaven, she appeared in the company of four of her ladies, in a kirtle of crimson, the color of the martyr, with a low-cut dress of gray damask cinched around her narrow waist, and a fur-trimmed robe, to submit to the "Sword of Calais," which her husband had decreed for her dispatch.

Never one to act in indecent haste, Henry waited until the following morning to announce his betrothal to Jane Seymour. Eleven days later, on May 30, she became Queen Number Three.

☙ Inside the citadel

The beautiful cold heart of the Tower of London is the White Tower, founded by William the Conqueror in 1078. A formidable example of Norman military architecture, it was built to guard London, to stand sentinel over the river, and to overawe and subdue the natives. Its inner and outer wards are surrounded by giant walls, with 20 mighty towers and bastions. It has never lost its power to overawe, or to subdue.

By its split personality, the Tower confounds the imagination. It was a royal palace, stronghold and arsenal, even as it was a monumental crime scene, a prison, and a place of bloody execution. Here were pageants and imprisonments, banquets and beheadings, song and dance and torture. Here, in the Garden Tower, renamed the Bloody Tower, the boy king, Edward V, and his brother, Richard, were last seen alive. They disappeared in 1483, *maybe* murdered by their usurping uncle Richard III. Although this was before Henry VIII's birth, the boys were his maternal uncles. It would strike us today as a tasteless, inauspicious place to fete one's new queen, as Henry did Anne.

This is all the more astonishing when we consider the superstition in which Tudor society was steeped. Henry believed in divine retribution—not for any of his heinous doings, but for inadvertence, for those matters in which he was in his innocence misguided or deceived. Despite bitter experience, he consulted astrologers. Witchcraft was a fact of life. His parliament would pass statutes condemning false prophesy, enchantment, the conjuration or invocation of spirits, and the use of sorcery "to find money or treasure or to waste, consume or destroy any person in his body members, or [shades of Anne Boleyn] to provoke any person to unlawful love." And yet he had no concept of bad karma, no sense that there was anything ill-starred or remotely inappropriate in his enjoyment of the Tower or the weird juxtaposition of the magnificent and the macabre.

It assists our understanding to realize that "the Tower" was not a single edifice but a kind of fortress village that fulfilled many roles. The Royal Wardrobe building—reduced today to a stump—provided storage for quantities of Henry's treasures, tapestries, carpets, gold plate, jewelry, robes, and all the other valuables by which he measured his magnificence. Important documents were kept in both the Royal Wardrobe and the White Tower.

In the Royal Menagerie, within the semicircular Lion Tower, four-legged prisoners must have been half-crazed by their loss of liberty, in cages barely six by ten feet. Many had been gifts to Henry, displayed for the titillation and curiosity of his court. The first record of lions at the Tower

BELOW: *The iconic White Tower is the oldest medieval building in the Tower complex, begun as a mighty fortress in 1078 by William the Conqueror to overawe the citizens of his conquered capital.*

was in 1210, during the reign of King John, who already had a Royal Menagerie at Woodstock. In 1235 John's son Henry III received three big cats as a gift from the Holy Roman Emperor. The beasts, known as "leopards," were Barbary lions. Three years later the king of France sent an elephant. The king of Norway made a gift of a polar bear, which used to fish for salmon in the Thames, on a chain. Henry VIII contributed a new acquisition, the turkey cock: an exotic, strutting bird that puffed out its chest, and proved very good to eat.

Secure within Tower precincts, the Royal Mint was kept busy coining Henry's sovereigns, ryals, crowns, angels and angelets, groats, shillings, farthings, George nobles, and testoons. The legend "Fid Def" (*Fidei Defensor*, Defender of the Faith) appeared on the coinage from 1521, when Pope Leo conferred the title on Henry. It has been used by every monarch since—Defender, that is, of the Church of England, not, as Pope Leo X had envisaged, the Church of Rome.

On Henry's accession in 1509, the post of die-engraver was held by the respected Alexander of Bruchsal. He was soon removed from the job to be replaced by one John Sharp, as part of Henry's "jobs for the boys" policy. On Sharp's death the sinecure passed to Henry Norris, who remained in office until 1936, when his associations with the Tower ended so bloodily.

In November 1534, the Act of Supremacy removed from the bishops the right of striking coins at ecclesiastical mints in Canterbury, York, and Durham. This was just part of a sustained campaign to undermine the Church's power and to tap into its wealth, to enrich the Crown, which would now have all the revenues. When the Dissolution of the Monasteries was at its height, confiscated gold and silver plate arrived at the Tower by the ton, to be melted down, with the Mint going hammer and tongs, both day and night.

Even so, by 1542, Henry was running low on funds and ordered the debasement of the currency whereby "silver" coins would be largely base metal. The fact that the silver often rubbed off the high relief of Henry's image to reveal the copper beneath earned him the derisive nickname "Old Copper Nose."

Earlier debasement, in 1526, had been designed to protect the national money supply and the viability of English mints. The Great Debasement had only one purpose: to raise money to feed Henry's addiction to war, his terror of invasion, and his passion for his much-expanded navy.

The authorized debasement was overseen by the Royal Mint's Master-Worker and Under-Treasurer, Sir Martin Bowes, who had valuable experience in the practice. Reorganization of the Royal Mint in 1544 revealed that even before debasement had become official, Bowes and colleague and

OPPOSITE: *By Tudor times the White Tower had become a military storehouse, but it had served as a prison up to the 15th century. This depiction recalls the incarceration by Henry V of Charles, Duke of Orléans, after the Battle of Agincourt in 1415. The illustration, dating from 1483, appeared in an illuminated manuscript of the duke's poems written in the Tower. He can be seen in the window, pen in hand.*

fellow goldsmith Ralph Rowlett had been responsible for debasement of silver supplied by the Crown, to their own advantage. Extraordinarily, Bowes kept both his head and his job.

Old coins were pouring in to be re-coined, and such was the pressure on production that bullion was stacking up, with delays of several months before new coins could be issued. To improve efficiency, the Royal Mint was divided into two independently working mints.

Whether through overwork or some malady, one William Foxley, pot-maker, fell asleep on the job, and for the next two weeks "could not be woken by pinching, cramping or otherwise burning whatsoever." Such was the fascination with the case that even Henry visited the Tower to take a look.

The coinages of Henry VIII could stand as a metaphor for his reign—from the gold angels minted upon his glorious accession to the debased testoons of his last years.

As Henry's early popularity dwindled and insurrection threatened, the Tower took on renewed importance as a military emplacement, armory, and stronghold. Unlike his pleasure palaces at Richmond and Greenwich, it had fearsome defensive capabilities. In 1536, with the Pilgrimage of Grace—a series of popular uprisings against his break with the Catholic Church and the Dissolution of the Monasteries—he seriously considered holing up there.

For many people today, the Tower of London always strikes a chill. The 20th-century writer VS Pritchett went so far as to suggest that it should be bulldozed as a symbol of cruelty and oppression. The sentiment is understandable, the proposition unthinkable. It would mean erasing from the London cityscape one of the most important collections of historic buildings in Britain. More than that, for Anne Boleyn's admirers and apologists it would mean the loss of the place above all where they pay their respects to Henry's second queen. It is here that she was buried without ceremony with her co-accused—in the Tower's parish church, the Chapel Royal of St Peter ad Vincula ("St Peter in Chains"), where the saint in chains keeps company with another saint, Sir Thomas More.

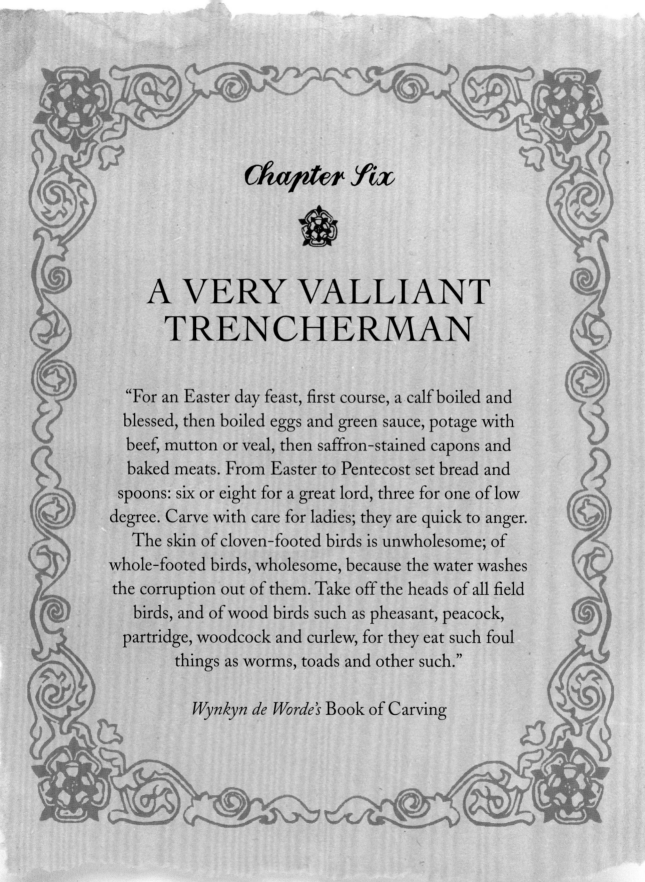

Chapter Six

A VERY VALLIANT TRENCHERMAN

"For an Easter day feast, first course, a calf boiled and blessed, then boiled eggs and green sauce, potage with beef, mutton or veal, then saffron-stained capons and baked meats. From Easter to Pentecost set bread and spoons: six or eight for a great lord, three for one of low degree. Carve with care for ladies; they are quick to anger. The skin of cloven-footed birds is unwholesome; of whole-footed birds, wholesome, because the water washes the corruption out of them. Take off the heads of all field birds, and of wood birds such as pheasant, peacock, partridge, woodcock and curlew, for they eat such foul things as worms, toads and other such."

Wynkyn de Worde's Book of Carving

As Henry prepares to dine in his Privy Chamber, the Ewerer for the King's Mouth lays a cloth of embroidered white linen before him, with ewers, fingerbowls, and basins of gold, glass, or marble, filled with water warmed in a chafing dish.

———————————

OPPOSITE: *Holbein's portrait of Henry upon his marriage to Jane Seymour—a companion to his portrait of Jane overleaf—shows how hefty Henry had become. No doubt he had a prodigious appetite for meat and drink, although even a king could not eat all the food that graced the royal board.*

*H*is Sewer (server), aided by the Carver, winds around him long strips of linen toweling. They set out manchets (fine-textured bread loaves made from a high-quality wheat flour and yeast) wrapped in a "coverpain" of gold-fringed silk, along with a type of sourdough known as cheat bread, which has a coarser texture and the yellow-gray color of wheat. Salt is precisely placed, with utensils of silver, ivory and jasper (knife, spoon, though not a fork—a fancy Italian affectation), a gold-fringed napkin, and trenchers of silver or marble. A further towel is draped over the king's shoulder and he is finally all swaddled and ready for a feast. From the Privy Kitchen below arrives a procession of senior officers, with Gentlemen Ushers at the rear bearing food on hefty serving dishes of silver-gilt.

The one-eyed Sir Francis Bryan is back in Club Henry as Chief Gentleman of the Privy Chamber. Sir Nicholas Carew is back, also; he is Master of the Horse. The original Mad Carew has calmed down since his wild youth; he and Bryan are trusted diplomats and intimates of His Majesty (a title Henry adopted to assert his equality with the French king and the Holy Roman Emperor).

It is the honeymoon period of June 1536 and Henry is in general a satisfied man. Troubled by an ulcerated leg, he has had to give up the joust—a bitter blow—but he has no intimation of impending tragedy, with the illness and death of his son, Henry FitzRoy, aged 17, a month away. He has a couple of projects on the go, about which he is excited. The Suppression of the Monasteries—grossly wealthy and corrupt institutions—is under way. Smaller monasteries with an annual income of less than £200 are to be closed and their property passed to the Crown. Full-scale Dissolution is looming; there are rich seams of ecclesiastical gold to be mined. Meanwhile, the king has the germ of an idea to build a new hunting lodge attached to Hampton Court, which will grow into a scheme for a brand new palace, modest in size but of such sumptuousness, artistry, and ostentation as the world has never seen.

He is enamored of his "first true wife." (Before Anne's execution, Thomas Cranmer had ruled marriage Number Two invalid.) In short, he manifests—in the callous words of Eustace Chapuys—"the joy and pleasure that a man feels in getting rid of a thin, vicious hack" and acquiring "a fine horse to ride."

✑ Plain Jane

A fine horse? Well, indeed a horse of quite another color. Jane Seymour could scarcely have been more different from Anne. She was born in around 1508, so was in her late 20s when she caught the king's eye. Precisely when their romance began, we do not know. One tends to discount tales of cat fights and blows between Anne and her maid Jane in the queen's Privy Chamber, or of Anne finding Jane perched on Henry's knee—such saucy behavior was more "Pretty Madge" Shelton's style.

Jane's father, Sir John Seymour, of Wolfhall in Wiltshire, was a Gentleman of the Bedchamber. He had sired six sons and four daughters with his wife, Margaret, or Margery, Wentworth, suggesting good breeding stock. Margaret was a descendant of Plantagenet kings, the warriors Edward I and III, and the lamentable Edward II. Jane's brother Edward had been made an Esquire of the Body to Henry; he was a Privy Chamber insider, as another brother, Thomas would be.

To modern eyes, Mistress Seymour lacked the siren charms of Anne Boleyn. In Hans Holbein's portrait she appears humorless and austere, in a gable hood à la Katharine of Aragon, whom she served before being passed on to Anne. Her jewelry throws her plainness into high relief, giving the lie to a remark by Sir John Russell, 1st Earl of Bedford, that the richer Queen Jane was in apparel, the fairer she appeared, while the opposite was true of Anne. The hood's lappets, or side flaps, are turned up, which gives a lift to the rather stolid face. The eyes are dark and pleasingly shaped. The upper lip is weak; this is not a mouth shaped for kissing. There is a hint of a double chin. If she "paints" she does so very subtly, for there is scant trace of makeup; Count Castiglione would approve.

Even Chapuys, who favored the marriage, was sparing with his praise, but he may, in his canny way, have put his finger on Queen Jane's appeal to the king. "She is of middle stature and no great beauty… The said Seymoure is not a woman of great wit, but she may have good understanding." The complaint of the faithless husband throughout history is, "My wife doesn't understand me," but for Henry, finally, here was a wife who did.

Jane also looks, in Holbein's painting, as if she knows more than she is telling. What she ought to have known, or must have strongly suspected, was that Anne was innocent of the charges contrived against her by her enemies. And those five men, Anne's alleged lovers and co-conspirators, Henry's erstwhile friends and confidants, were therefore sacrificial lambs. Chapuys had the honesty to admit that Anne had been "condemned upon presumption and certain indications" without valid proof. There were, he intimated,

ABOVE: *Henry's other half. Holbein's complementary portraits of the king and Jane Seymour were once together, hinged to close like a book, face to face. The couple share a look, not of elation, but of unhappy distraction.*

murmurs against the "mode of procedure" of her trial, and "it will not pacify the world when it is known what has passed and is passing between [the king] and Mrs Jane Semel."

Jane Seymour had had an understanding with Henry that she would be the next queen. She had had an apartment at Greenwich Palace, chaperoned by her brother Edward and his wife, where Henry could visit her by some backstairs route, unobserved. The 17th-century historian Thomas Fuller told the story that Jane wore about her neck a jeweled locket, and that Anne one day, making a grab for it, "hurt her hand with her own violence, but it grieved her heart more, when she perceived in it the king's picture by himself bestowed upon her, who from this day forward dated her own declining and the other's ascending, in her husband's affection."

Both Henry and Jane had set their hearts on marriage, but first the means had had to be found to bring Anne down. Cromwell was in on it. Bryan was in on it. Carew was in on it. Jane Seymour was complicit at the very least by default.

Five centuries on, we may read in her visage the stony determination with which she had seen the project through to its conclusion—or the passivity of a queen who chose the motto "Bound to Obey and Serve."

ℨ Cooking for king and court

But it is morning at Hampton Court, and Henry is waiting to eat. "Hours certain to be kept for dynner and supper" were laid down by Wolsey: "First dinner to begin at ten of the clock, and supper at four of the clock… and on Holy Days the first dinner to begin at eleven of the clock in the forenoon… and supper at six o'clock in the afternoon."

The vast kitchen complex has been in action since before first light, chimneys smoking, bellows puffing, cauldrons bubbling, dough rising, cheat and manchet loaves baking in the Bakehouse, fish salting in the Dry Fish House, meats pickling, sauces seething in the Saucery, pottages simmering. Pastry cooks and confectioners are practicing their exquisite arts. Scullions scrub and scour. Deliveries of sacks, vats, butts, hogsheads, barrels, and bottles are counted in and checked for weight and quality. The toil and

ABOVE: *A fireplace at the restored Tudor kitchens of Hampton Court Palace. Meat and game would have been roasted over the flames, and fish grilled over the embers. For the cooks charged with turning the spits, it was punishing work.*

hubble-bubble will continue through to evening, with the cutting up of meat for the morrow, when the labors will begin all over again, with some 800 mouths to be fed.

The entire kitchen enterprise is a masterwork of organization. The Privy and Great Wine Cellars, the Beer Cellar, the Dry and Wet Larders are all stocked. A clerk is drawing up his list of a month's supplies for the Spicery, Confectionery, Chandlery, Wafery, Ewery, and Laundry. Another is projecting the week's requirement for the Pantries, Poultry, Buttery, the Woodyard, and the Pastry House. The Chief Clerk of the kitchen, with his two under-clerks, must ensure "especially that stuff of victuals as pertaineth to the king's dish be of the best and sweetest that can be got." Good value is assured by compulsory purchase from suppliers at below market prices.

The nerve center is the Counting House, where the "White Sticks" take charge of administration. The Lord Steward, George Talbot, Earl of Shrewsbury, an old military hand, has been commander in chief for 34 years; he knows the job backward. He is assisted by the Treasurer and Controller of the Household, Sir William FitzWilliam and Sir William Paulet, and a cofferer. They must ensure that all departments run smoothly, that everything is replenished, that money is not wasted nor resources plundered. Every spoon must be accounted for. From beyond the grave, Thomas Wolsey admonishes the Sergeant of the Squillery (scullery) "to see his vessels, as well silver as pewter, be well and truly kept and saved from losses and stealing… King's purveyors of wines to see to the provision of the best wines at the best price, for the king's most profit and advantage… and they do not embezzle [waste], sell or put away any part of the same provisions."

So, in his Privy Chamber Henry sits, remote from the turmoil, anticipating his repast. Contrary to popular perception, he is a decorous eater. There is no tearing into chicken legs with his teeth and tossing the bones over his shoulder to packs of salivating dogs. For one thing, Wolsey banished greyhounds, mastiffs, and the like to "kennels and other meet places" so the house should be "sweet and wholesome"—though "a few small spaniels for ladies" are countenanced. In the court of King Henry, manners maketh man—and woman. We have to hope that those backsliding courtiers who once "cast vessels abroad out of their chambers, laying any manner of dishes, platters, saucers and leftovers in galleries or at their chamber doors" have mended their ways.

So, what will Henry eat today? A lot!

ABOVE: *Baking was a great part of the cooks' work, with constant demand for bread, meat pies, and sweet pastries. "Open hot meat pies at the top," advises Wynkyn de Worde, "cold in the middle." The opening of a pie demanded caution when, as a party piece, the crust was broken and live birds came fluttering out.*

❦ Conspicuous consumption

The English take great pleasure in having a quantity of excellent victuals, and also of remaining a long time at table… Being great epicures, they are very avaricious by nature, indulge in the most delicate fare themselves, and give their household the coarsened bread and beer, and cold meat baked on Sunday for the week, of which they allow them in great abundance.

An Italian envoy, writing in around 1500, described very neatly how it was in the Tudor court. Meals were gargantuan. Even the most menial servants had plenty of sustenance—enjoying a healthier regimen, in truth, than that of the nobles, and many times more healthy than the sovereign's. For, with everyone catered to according to their rank, and with the show of plenty an essential aspect of magnificence, the king and queen had to confront some seriously daunting belly-cheer twice daily.

Fish and meat made up the largest part of the fare, and anything on the wing, on the hoof, or on the hop was fair game for the oven, spit, griddle or pot. As one 19th-century writer wryly commented, it was as if the purveyors of the table went over Christendom with a dragnet.

Here, distilled from the Eltham Ordinances, is a "declaration of… the diett for the King's majesty and the Queen's grace, of like fare" for a flesh day (Sunday to Thursday).

Dinner: cheat bread and manchet, beer and ale, wine, pottage, chine of beef, venison, pasties of red deer, mutton, young veal, swan, goose, stork, capon or cony, flounders, baked carp, custard garnished or fritters.

So much for starters, now on to the main course. Jelly, ipocras (spiced and sugared red wine), cream of almonds, pheasant, heron, bittern, shoveler, partridges, quails, cocks, plovers or gulls, kid, lamb or pigeon, larks or rabbit, snipe, pullet or chicken.

For supper, not so very many hours later, would be cheat bread and manchet, beer and wine, pottage, chickens, sparrow or lamb stewed, with chine of mutton, gigot of mutton or venison "stopped with cloves," capons, cony, pheasant, heron, shoveler, cocks, plovers or gulls, sweet dowcets or oranges, quinces of pippins. Main course: blancmange (pounded poultry boiled with milk and almonds, sweetened with honey or sugar), kid, lamb or pigeon, partridge or quails, godwit or teals, pullets, rabbits or larks, tarte, fruit, venison or other baked meats.

Birds for the table included the great bustard (extinct by the 1830s and since reintroduced), egret, curlew, and peacock. Peacock and swan would be displayed in lifelike form, dressed in their feathers and with heads intact. "It is a truly beautiful thing," wrote the Venetian ambassador, "to behold two thousand tame swans upon the river Thames, which are eaten by the English like duck and geese. Nor do they dislike, which we abominate, crows, rooks and jackdaws." A party trick to amuse honored guests was to cut open a pastry crust and watch small birds flutter out.

For fish days—Friday, Saturday, and Lent—the spread was similarly lavish, with fish from sea and river, lake and stew pond, including sole, plaice, flounder, turbot, and halibut, quantities of ling, mullet, eels and lampreys, sturgeon, whiting, haddock, carp, pike, perch, crabs and lobsters, shrimps and crayfish, mullet, salmon, smelts, gurnard, pike, perch, tench… There were, too, some decidedly queer fish, including beaver's tail, porpoise, and seal, as well as puffins, the last being "Birds in show and Fish in substance, or, as one might justly call them, feathered Fishes… permitted by Popes to be eaten at Lent." The rarest of all, mentioned in one contemporary book on fish, and probably never served at court, was the siren, or mermaid, "a deadly beast that brought a man gladly to death, from the navel up like a woman, with a dreadful face… and is like the eagle in the nether parts… with great hanging breasts."

Potatoes, tomatoes, and bananas were unknown, but the turkey cock was introduced to the British repertoire, and new ingredients were making their way from the New World, including many varieties of bean (the fava, or broad bean, was the only variety to make the journey from Old World to New). Sugar cost a fortune, so elaborate sugar sculptures and confections were not just objects of beauty but statements of prosperity.

Although, with the years, Henry increasingly preferred to take his meals in his Privy Chamber, when extending hospitality to important guests, he would preside at the top table in the Presence Chamber, seated on a dais, under a golden canopy.

Trumpets summoned to the board men and women of every estate, to be served "according to their degree," so that lesser mortals had merely a tantalizing whiff of the finest food being borne past them by liveried servers. Although rules were mainly concerned with rich apparel, there were sumptuary laws designed to guard against excessive fare at feasts (other, of course, than the king's). From 1517, the number of dishes served was to be

OPPOSITE: *"Break that deer, lift that swan, sauce that capon, truss that chicken, dismember the heron, display the crane, wing the partridge, mince the plover, thigh the pigeon, chine the salmon, string the lamprey, splat that pike, barbe the lobster…"* Wynkyn de Worde's instructions to cooks and carvers convey the superabundance of meat and game, fish and fowl.

regulated according to the rank of the highest person present. Feasts were preceded by a "warner," and each course was followed up with a "subtlety." These were edible and inedible ornamental confections made, for instance, of sugar, plaster, and board, which towered above the table, brightly painted and gilded. A menu for a celebratory meal for the king and queen and Knights of the Garter contains such oddities as "A George on horseback," "custard planted with garters," "porpoise in armor," "birds of the nest," and "a tarte closed with arms."

George Cavendish cherished memories of one special feast given by Wolsey at Hampton Court, its purpose to overwhelm guests from France. Such was the accompanying music that the Frenchmen were "rapt into a heavenly paradise." The cardinal arrived late in order to make an entrance. He appeared booted and spurred "all suddenly," as the first course was cleared, "and straight away… sat himself down in the midst of the table, laughing and being merry as ever I saw him in all my life." Cavendish goes on to describe the second course:

…with so many dishes, subtleties and curious devices, which were about a hundred in number, of so good proportion and costly, that I suppose the Frenchmen never saw the like… There were castles with images of the same, Paul's Church and Steeple… beasts, birds, fowls of divers kinds, and personages most lively, made and counterfeited in dishes, some

fighting… with swords, some with guns and crossbows, some vaulting and leaping, some dancing with ladies… Among all I noted there was a chessboard subtly made of spiced plate, with men to the same…

Wolsey took a golden bowl filled with ipocras, and so many toasts were drunk that "many of the Frenchmen were fain to be led to bed." The next day the party moved to Greenwich, where, in the tiltyard banqueting chamber, the hospitality exceeded even that at Hampton Court, "the same as fine gold doth silver."

So the days passed for Henry, as the weight piled on, and in March 1537 came the news for which the nation had been hoping and praying. Queen Jane was eating for two.

✠ The lord giveth…

Jane Seymour was no enchantress or sorceress, but early in her marriage to Henry she had wrought a little white magic, urging for rapprochement with Katharine's daughter, Princess Mary. That sad, forlorn girl had lost her

RIGHT: **The Family of Henry VIII** *painted by an unknown artist and now on display at Hampton Court, shows Henry enthroned at Whitehall Palace, with his son grown to boyhood, his wife Jane still at his side. Mary and Elizabeth stand a little distanced to denote their illegitimacy. In the arch on the right we see the king's jester Will Somers; in the left-hand arch, possibly, Jane Fool, a female jester.*

mother, but she would return to the fold and to the love of a father who would have seen her in the Tower for her insolence to Anne. For that kindness alone Jane deserves to be honored.

She furthermore displayed many characteristics vaunted by Giuliano de' Medici in Castiglione's *The Book of the Courtier*. That is, to be "mannerly, clever, prudent, not arrogant, not slanderous, not vain, not quarrelsome, not silly." Since "women are imperfect creatures, and consequently of less dignity than men," averred de' Medici, and "since nature always aims and designs to make things most perfect, [the ideal lady courtier] should continually bring forth men… and when a woman is born, it is a defect or mistake of nature."

In late September Jane took to her chamber for her confinement, secure in the knowledge that her unborn child was no defect or mistake of nature, and that she would bring forth a prince—as solemnly promised by the astrologers.

The itinerary had been drawn up for a progress to the north that summer, but Henry, doubtless unnerved by the Pilgrimage of Grace and fearful of his feisty northern barons, had cancelled it, giving as his reason

concern for "our most dear and most entirely beloved wife, the Queen, now quick with child." According to the revised plan, he would progress no farther than 60 miles.

In the small hours of October 12, 1537, at Hampton Court Palace, after 60 hours of labor, Jane gave birth to the only child she would ever bear. "Trust and well-beloved," she wrote to Henry in a beautiful hand, "we greet you well. And forasmuch as by the inestimable goodness and grace of Almighty God, we be delivered and brought in childbed of a Prince…" Henry had waited 28 years, but finally he had a male heir. He took him in his arms and wept.

Three days later, the boy, wrapped in velvet and fur, was christened Edward after his great-grandfather, Edward IV. Bells rang out in steeples across the land, bonfires blazed, and wine flowed. Princess Mary acted as godmother to the infant who had supplanted her as Henry's heir. Edward Seymour bore the four-year-old Elizabeth in his arms. This was a family united.

Then Jane began to fail. Like Henry's mother, Elizabeth of York, she was succumbing to "childbed sickness." For a few days it seemed that her fighting spirit would prevail, but by the morning of October 24 she was sinking. Before midnight she had died.

The funeral was on November 12. Jane was buried in St George's Chapel at Windsor Castle. For Princess Mary, this new bereavement was almost more than she could endure—she was crazed with sorrow, though no one was more stricken with grief than Henry.

At Hampton Court there is a painting, made in 1545 by an unknown artist, in the style of Holbein (previous pages). Entitled *The Family of Henry VIII*, it shows the king seated at the center, under a splendid canopy, with the boy Edward, aged eight, at his right hand, his queen at his left. Off to either side stand his daughters, Mary and Elizabeth, regal and poised. Behind them, arches frame views of the Great Garden at Whitehall Palace, with the gilded King's Beasts amid flowerbeds marked out with fencing in Tudor colors, clearly visible. The work is an affecting piece of wishfulness, a study of what might have been. Henry, by this time a decrepit monster not two years from death, appears to be in his prime, a fine if hefty figure of a man. And the Queen who sits so demurely with her hands in her lap is not Catherine Parr, the survivor, but Jane Seymour.

It is often said that Jane was the wife that "Henry really loved," which ignores the love that he felt for Katharine over years of marriage. If Jane had lived, who knows? His love might have waned. Some other young and pretty maid might have taken his fancy.

PARVVLE PATRISSA, PATRIÆ VIRTVTIS ET HÆRES
ESTO, NIHIL MAIVS MAXIMVS ORBIS HABET.
GNATVM VIX POSSVNT CŒLVM ET NATVRA DEDISSE,
HVIVS QVEM PATRIS, VICTVS HONORET HONOS.
ÆQVATO TANTVM, TANTI TV FACTA PARENTIS,
VOTA HOMINVM, VIX QVO PROGREDIANTVR, HABENT
VINCITO, VICISTI. QVOT REGES PRISCVS ADORAT
ORBIS, NEC TE QVI VINCERE POSSIT, ERIT.

The truth is that five times out of six Henry, an incurable romantic, married for love. Before Jane was even in the ground, Thomas Cromwell was working on the question of who would be wife Number Four—the exception.

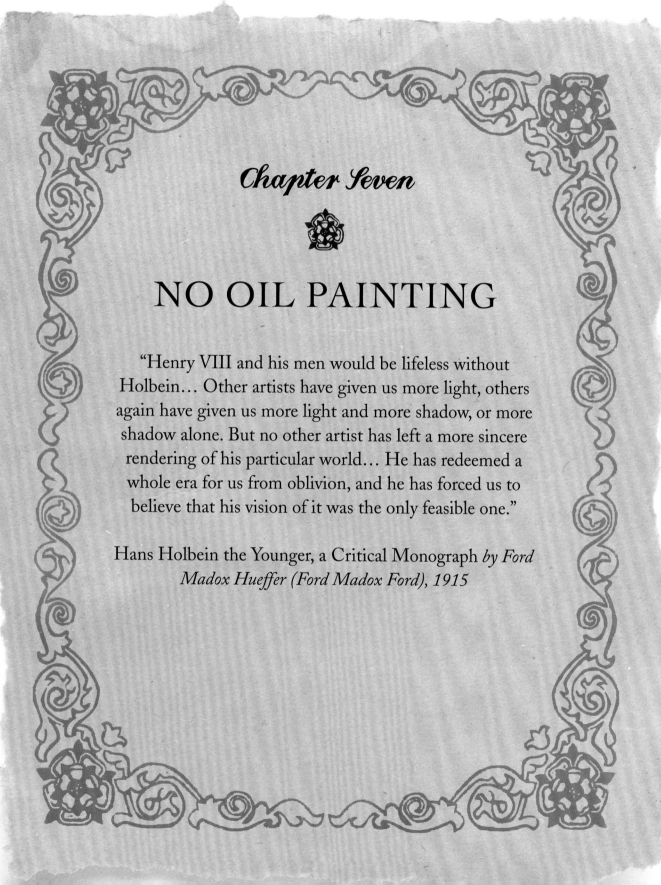

Chapter Seven

NO OIL PAINTING

"Henry VIII and his men would be lifeless without Holbein… Other artists have given us more light, others again have given us more light and more shadow, or more shadow alone. But no other artist has left a more sincere rendering of his particular world… He has redeemed a whole era for us from oblivion, and he has forced us to believe that his vision of it was the only feasible one."

Hans Holbein the Younger, a Critical Monograph *by Ford Madox Hueffer (Ford Madox Ford), 1915*

"I like her not!" Henry's reaction to his fourth bride was immediate and brutal. Thomas Cromwell was the master of the black arts of spin and espial. He had helped the king to extricate himself from his first marriage, winning his favor, but in acting as fixer for his fourth he got it fatally wrong.

***

OPPOSITE: *Holbein's original Whitehall mural depiction of Henry VIII, now destroyed, was one of the most influential portraits ever (see page 58). An unforgettable depiction of the swaggering plutocrat of popular imagination, his legs spread to bear his great weight, it inspired many imitations, mostly by unknown artists. This one, by an anonymous artist of the late 16th century, shows the king wearing a jeweled cap, gray slashed doublet, and scarlet gown trimmed with fur.*

After the death of Queen Jane, notwithstanding the birth of a prince, Henry and his household were plunged into gloom. In the microclimate of court, the king was the weather, radiant sunshine, tempest, Arctic chill. Now it seemed winter was back to stay. For men such as Nicholas Carew, it must have recalled the last dark days of Henry VII.

The one glimmer of hope was that another wife could be found to perk up His Majesty. Everyone desired it. From the day that Henry ascended the throne there had been a queen—indeed, before he deserted Katharine, in all but name there had been two, the Queen of Hearts and the Queen of Diamonds. With no consort, the court lacked symmetry, balance, a feminine side. Where was the woman who could fill the vacancy? Cromwell was straight away on the case.

Unlike most of his peers in European princedom, Henry had so far had his choice of wives. Now was his opportunity to marry a princess from France or the Holy Roman Empire, shoring up an alliance with Francis I or Charles V, to the exclusion and vexation of one or the other.

On October 31, 1537, Cromwell, while blaming Jane's attendants for her demise ("who suffered her to take cold and eat such things as her fantasy in sickness called for"), had his sights trained across the Channel. The king might be "little disposed to marry again," but, Cromwell ruminated, "two persons in France might be thought on, viz, the French king's daughter (said to be not the meetest) and Madame de Longueville."

The Duchess of Longueville, Mary of Guise, was the widow of Louis II d'Orléans. Like Henry, she was recently bereaved and, encouragingly, the mother of an infant son. She was strikingly tall, accomplished, with feminine grace. She was also pledged to Henry's nephew, the 25-year-old James V of Scotland.

On November 3, as preparations for Jane's funeral were in hand, Cromwell exhorted Henry to accept her death as God's will, to take comfort in his son, and, for the sake of the realm, "to provide for a new wife." Henry was sufficiently taken with the possibilities to propose that some form of beauty

ABOVE: *Henry hankered to wed Mary of Guise, the tall, young, and beautiful widow of Louis II d'Orléans, Duke of Longueville. Henry told the French ambassador that, as a big man, he needed a big wife. Mary's response was to quote Anne Boleyn (she might be big, she said, "but I have a very little neck")—and to marry Henry's upstart nephew, the Scottish king.*

pageant be staged for him in Calais, a suggestion that would provoke Francis I to snort that the English "meant to do with women as they do with their geldings, collect a number and trot them out to take which goes best." He was particularly offended by the idea that his daughter, the 14-year-old Marguerite of Valois, should be "put in a row with the others."

How a bevy of nubile princesses and duchesses might have felt about marrying a 46-year-old paunchy gorbelly with a reputation as a wife-killer one can only surmise, but none of them would have had a veto if it had been decided for her.

Officially, Francis was gracious, his answer indicating that he had received Cromwell's overtures in good part. He intimated that he would regard it as an honor if Henry took a wife in France, "and there is no lady who is not at his commandment except Madame de Longueville."

Nothing could have more surely piqued Henry's desire. The perennial child who must have his own way, he could not accept that this paragon was unavailable to him. On December 30, the French Ambassador, Louis de Perreau, Sieur de Castillon, wrote to Francis that "he is so amorous… that he cannot refrain from coming back upon it. I assured him that the marriage between the king of Scots and her had been already sworn." Castillon had tried to tease Henry out of his fixation, asking, "Would you marry another man's wife?" But Henry persisted: Castillon must write at once to ask if the betrothal could be annulled.

The next day a secretary of the king came to inform the Frenchman that Cromwell had learned from one of his agents in France that the lady had never promised to marry the Scottish king, and therefore Francis must grant her to Henry. If the answer was no, they would need to know why; King Henry must not think himself refused, only to gratify the king of Scotland.

By mid-February, Henry was in foot-stamping mode. Castillon wrote to Francis that "he was surprised you refused her to him to deliver her to his enemy, and were it not that he wished to remain your good brother and ally, everything gives him occasion to be suspicious."

While this charade was playing out, the English court was officially still in mourning for the "entirely beloved" Jane. At Easter, Lady Kingston requested of Cromwell that he ask Henry if she "should leave wearing black" and don her "white taffeta edged with velvet… for this joyful feast of our Lord's holy rising from the dead."

Lady Kingston's garb was surely a matter of indifference to Henry, consumed as he was with frustrated desire for a woman he had never met. For himself, he ordered a violet coat trimmed with marten fur as he dreamed of cutting a fine figure for his French bride.

In mid-May, five days after Mary became Mrs James V, he was still harping on to Castillon, protesting that he had always desired peace with his brother Francis—even wishing to take a wife in France—but apparently Francis preferred his enemies, the Pope and the king of the Scots.

Castillon assured him that Francis would let him choose any other woman in his kingdom. In fact, why not Mary's sister, the very image of Mary, a young lady as beautiful, talented, and graceful as Madame de Longueville? What was more, he added with a verbal dig in the ribs, the young woman was a virgin: Henry would have the advantage of… let us say, shaping her to his will. Henry chuckled, clapped him on the shoulder and went away "with a good countenance."

For all his threats, sulks, and pleading over Mary, Henry had meanwhile had his eye on another match entirely, with Christina, Duchess of Milan, aged 16. The daughter of Christian II of Denmark and Isabella of Austria, and niece of Charles V, she, too, was a widow, having been married at 12 or 13, by proxy, to the Duke of Milan.

Christina was raised by her aunt, the Dowager Queen Mary of Hungary, Governor of the Netherlands. The ambassador John Hutton had written to Cromwell from Brussels, describing Christina as "reportedly of good personage and of excellent beauty." At Christmas he was able to avow at first hand: "She is very tall… of competent beauty, soft of speech, and gentle in countenance. She wears mourning after the manner of Italy… She is said to be both widow and maid. She resembles one Mrs Shelton that used to wait on Queen Anne." Christina spoke French—another plus—with a slight lisp, "which does not misbecome her." To Cromwell's secretary, Thomas Wriothesley, Hutton wrote, "She is not so pure white as the late Queen… but she hath a singular good countenance, and when she chanceth to smile there appeareth two pits in her cheeks, and one in her chin, the which becometh her right excellently well."

Sweet 16, a virgin, tall, with a dimply smile, the image of Madge Shelton… *and* she adored hunting and card games! What could have been more to Henry's taste? Her uncle, the Holy Roman Emperor, professed

RIGHT: *Another very eligible—and very young—widow and possible bride was Christina of Denmark, Duchess of Milan. Like Mary of Guise, she did not choose to stick her neck out. Holbein's portrait of her hangs in the National Gallery. "I would rather possess this painting than any other object in the world," declared the writer Ford Madox Ford.*

himself broadly in favor, as "many things could be done for the good of Christendom" thereby—but Henry had better get a move on! Henry's children were to be factored in as a form of collateral. The imperial ambassadors would agree, wrote Chapuys to Mary of Hungary, if Princess Mary were promised to Don Louis of Portugal, Elizabeth to the Duke of Savoy, and Prince Edward to Charles V's second daughter.

Henry wanted the best possible political advantage—and the best possible dowry terms. But, even more, he wanted the fairest of them all. Verbal descriptions served a limited purpose. He naturally desired to see with his own eyes. And if he could not have these pretty foreign fillies lined up and trotted before him, he must have the next best thing: paintings. Happily, at court there was the very man for the job.

❧ Mr Haunce

Ars longa, vita brevis. Art is long, life is short. Thanks to the enduring work of one singular painter, five centuries later Henry's courtiers are vivid in the mind's eye. The German artist Hans Holbein the Younger had come to England from Lutheran Basle in 1526 with a letter of recommendation from Erasmus to Thomas More. He returned in 1532, to work under the patronage of Anne Boleyn and Thomas Cromwell, and was appointed King's Painter three years later. It is as if, with his arrival, a theater curtain was lifted to reveal the central players in the drama that was the life of Henry VIII. How would we manage without him?

The first truly "alive" portrait that we have of Henry (excluding Lucas Horenbout's miniatures from 1525) was painted by Holbein to celebrate the king's marriage to Jane. Viewed side by side, each appears to be dwelling on some inner sadness. They do not look like a couple celebrating their "happiest day."

It was Holbein's job, not to flatter but to immortalize—to capture the outward aspect of the sitter, the shape of nose and chin, the curl of mouth, the shade of hair. It was his genius to capture their essence. He did not spend weeks peering into their souls. He would make, in a few hours, a silverpoint sketch with thin washes of color, dash off some detail of ornament, scribble a few succinct notes, and then go away to paint in oils, from his extraordinarily visual memory.

Since we have no means of knowing for sure, but hear no suggestions to the contrary, we have to trust that his intense, cerebral Thomas More, his sly and fleshy Thomas Cromwell, his lean, ethereal, faintly humorous Erasmus are as their loved ones would have recognized them. Holbein's Thomas More is a man with a vision of a better world, Utopia; his Thomas Cromwell is

absolutely earthbound. Thomas Howard, 3rd Duke of Norfolk, is full of trouble—as well he might be. The weary old man William Warham, Archbishop of Canterbury, has seen more than he can endure. In Holbein's sketch of John Fisher, the martyred bishop might be not so much coming into being as evanescent, fading out of it. The work was probably done in the Tower, where Fisher had the leisure to reflect on Warham's maxim: "the King's anger is death."

The year 1538 was a busy one for the maestro. On March 10, Hutton wrote to Cromwell that "a servant of the King named Haunce" had arrived and that Christina had agreed to a portrait. In the three hours that were granted to him, Holbein had made his sketch. The resulting painting had shown him to be "master of that science, for it is very perfect." When Henry was presented with the standing portrait, "being her whole stature," he was champing at the bit. He would have no qualms about wedding and bedding his first wife's great-niece; nor did he give a fig for William, the young Duke of Cleves, to whom Christina was already tentatively betrothed. As to this young woman's own feelings, she is said to have remarked that if she'd had two heads, the king of England could have one of them. Pressed for a less facetious response, she replied that she was "at the Emperor's commandment."

Toadying Wriothesley assured her that Henry was "the most gentle Gentleman that liveth, his nature so benign and pleasant, that I think till this day no man hath heard many angry words pass his mouth." At those words Christina appeared "tickled"—moved to delight.

In early June, Holbein traveled to France to make paintings of Francis I's daughter Marguerite, and of another contender, Marie de Vendôme. On the next trip he was, by means of absurd subterfuge, to portray Renée and Louise, younger sisters of Mary of Guise, and their cousin Anne of Lorraine. One way or another this would all come to nothing. On June 17, the Emperor and Francis signed a ten-year truce, which, though it would prove hollow, left Henry feeling like the odd man out.

The haggling over Christina continued nonetheless. In October, Sir Thomas Wyatt, by now ambassador to the Imperial court, opined that the Emperor was dissimulating to keep Henry in suspense and to demonstrate to the world that he had the English king waiting on his decision. The Duchess, he said, had secretly been offered in marriage to "France and other places." Mulishly, Henry continued to send ambassadors to press his suit.

The months rolled on, with the parties still "busy brewing marriages," as the French ambassador, Castillon, put it. In September John Hutton died, no nearer to a satisfactory outcome. On December 17, Pope Paul III excommunicated Henry. Christmas came and went. In late January Castillon wrote begging to be recalled to France, suggesting that Henry had lost his mind, and fearing for his safety in the court of "the most dangerous and cruel man in the world."

Then, finally, during Lent 1539, Charles V played his Ace of Spades, the death card to Henry's hopes, insisting that his marriage would require dispensation from the Pope.

More than 16 months had been wasted, and with Henry no closer to finding a wife, Thomas Cromwell's lizard eyes swiveled in another direction.

❧ Very lively expressed

The Duchy of Cleves, in the patchwork territory of the Lower Rhine, was a state of the Holy Roman Empire. It was Protestant, but was ruled, until his death in February 1539, by the Duke of Cleves, John III, a well-read and enlightened man known as "the Peaceful," who believed in a "middle way." The guiding influence was not Martin Luther, but Erasmus.

With his wife, Maria of Jülich-Berg, Duke John had had four children, Sibylle, Anne (born September 22, 1515), William, and Amalia. Sibylle was already married, so it was with Anne and Amalia in mind that Richard Berde and Nicholas Wotton sailed from England in May 1539. Duke John III's heir, William, was happy to entertain the prospect of a great marriage for one of his sisters. There were said to be portraits of both, painted some six months earlier, which were to be made available, but the envoys insisted they must be shown the young women, to judge the likeness of their images. Rather grudgingly, then, Anne and Amalia were presented to the Englishmen, in some "monstrous habit and apparel" that revealed "neither their faces nor their persons." "Why," came the shocked reply from the Duchy's Chancellor to the protesting visitors, "would you see them naked?" So Henry's painter was on the move again.

In August, Wotton sent word home that "Hanze Albein" had arrived in the Duchy of Cleves to portray Anne and Amalia, and had "expressed their images very lively." When Henry was presented with an ivory box carved like a rose, containing Holbein's miniature of Anne, he was resolved to have her. He wrote to Duke William urging a swift conclusion, as winter was approaching. He had been a widower for nearly two years, an unnatural state for him, and he could not wait to meet his new bride, half his age.

Wait he would have to, however, as adverse weather prevented Anne from sailing from Calais until two days after Christmas. It was late at night when she came ashore at Deal in Kent, from where she was escorted by torchlight to Dover Castle, before traveling onward to Canterbury. On the last day of the old year she was received at Rochester, at the Bishop's Palace, where Henry planned to spring himself upon her by way of a surprise. The visit, he told Cromwell, was "to nourish love." Instead, once he had met her, he felt worse than disappointed. He'd been misled! Cheated! Sold a pup! He would grumble to Sir Anthony Browne, his Master of the Horse, "I see nothing in this woman as men report of her." To Cromwell he seethed, "Had I known as much before as I know now, she would never have come into this realm."

How had the deft and visionary Holbein so beguiled the king with that infamous portrait? It has been alleged that he was pressured by Cromwell to

OPPOSITE: *While Holbein's portrait of Christina of Denmark so delighted Henry that he had his musicians play all day, his reaction to the artist's most infamous portrait must have been more muted. Holbein did not paint Anne of Cleves as a great beauty; she appears kind, capable, modest, in her richly collared clothing. The portrait now hangs in Paris in the Louvre.*

flatter his subject, but he was too true to himself for that. He did, though, have to compromise, to satisfy his hosts in Cleves, while producing for Henry as honest a rendering as he could.

In fact, while Anne was considered a beauty by her countrymen, she appears in Holbein's portrait quite plain. There is no attempt to pass her off as another Christina of Milan. Whatever Wotton thought, she lacks a pulse, and is swamped by her garments of rich red and gold and her heavy jewelry. The artist was too tactful even to hint at the smallpox scars—which none of Henry's emissaries, for that matter, had seen fit to mention.

Hans Holbein held Anne for three hours in his perspicacious, painterly regard, then went off and conjured an image that on the one hand would not cause offence, and on the other was not contrived to seduce. It may not have been a travesty, but it was to be Mr Haunce's last important royal commission.

❧ God Send Me Well to Keep

In thrall to chivalric romance, Henry VIII cherished a belief in love at first sight. Arriving at Rochester on the first day of 1540, he was in hope of a *coup de foudre* (a lightning strike to the heart). He and five men of his Privy Chamber were disguised in varicolored coats and masks, and Henry carried a gift for his new bride, a "partlett furred with sables and sable skins for her neck, with a muffler furred and a cap."

According to Wriothesley, Henry ascended to the Privy Chamber where he found Anne at the window, watching bull-baiting in the courtyard below. "Suddenly he embraced her and kissed her, and showed her a token that the king had sent for her New Year gift, and she, being abashed, not knowing who it was, thanked him, and so he communed with her, but she regarded him little, but always looked at the window at the bull-baiting."

The ingénue Anne, born into a very foreign culture and nurtured by her strait-laced mother, did not understand the rules of engagement. Henry had assumed that she would recognize his princely person—for who else would take the liberty of kissing her?—and swoon at his feet. Instead she let her attention stray repeatedly to the tormented bulls. Only when Henry left the room and returned in a coat of purple velvet, to be hailed by his nobles, did she "humble her grace lowly to the king's majesty."

Whatever her natural attributes—a "determined and resolute countenance" and "steadiness of purpose in her face" are impartial descriptions—Anne cannot have been looking her best. She had made a long voyage by land and sea. She was dressed in mourning for her father, was probably homesick, and was certainly exhausted (to the French ambassador, that night, she looked to be 30). Nothing had prepared her for her fiancé, whose trip had been by royal barge from Greenwich, down the Thames, with a short hop overland to come to her fresh as a daisy.

This disastrous first encounter set the scene for the marriage. Whether or not Henry truly described Anne as a "fat Flanders mare," she was far from his ideal, even had she been a beauty. She spoke only her native "Dutch" (*Deutsch*)—no English, French, or Latin. She liked to sew but could not sing or play an instrument, for, as Wotton had explained, "they take it here in Germany as a rebuke and an occasion of lightness that great ladies should be learned or have any knowledge of music." As to flirtation and courtly love, she had not a clue.

Henry might have extricated himself before it was too late. There was unresolved confusion over an earlier contract by which Anne's father had promised her to the son of the Duke of Lorraine—the documentary evidence of a get-out clause had not been forthcoming. There was, though, the national interest to consider. At the turn of the year, in Paris, the French king was feting the Holy Roman Emperor, on a march through France to put down an uprising in Ghent. Such cooperation was disquieting. Henry should not, Cromwell cautioned, "make a ruffle in the wind," for fear of alienating Duke William and driving him over to the side of the Catholic monarchs.

So while Francis I treated Charles V to "all the pleasures that can be invented, as royal hunts, tourneys, skirmishes, fights a-foot and a-horseback and all other sort of pastimes," Henry morosely anticipated his nuptials.

The wedding ceremony was to be held on Twelfth Night, January 6, 1540, in the Queen's Closet at Greenwich Palace, where he had married Jane. "My Lord," he confided to Cromwell, "if it were not to satisfy the world, and my realm, I would not do that I must do this day for none earthly thing." Anne chose for her queenly motto "God send me well to keep," which we might roughly translate as "God help me!"

According to Eustace Chapuys, the bride wore a "rich coronet of stone and pearls set with rosemary on her hair, and a gown of rich cloth of silver, richly hung with stones and pearls." Bride and groom processing together presented "a goodly sight to behold." But if any skeptic in the crowd was heard to mutter, "I give it six months," they were right on the money.

The following month, the Duke of Norfolk was dispatched to Paris for a meeting with Francis I, at which the Duke enticed Francis away from his entente with Charles V. Henry had married to satisfy the world and his realm. He need not have bothered. Now he was desperate to extricate himself—Anne of Cleves was anathema to him. And, besides, there had been a second epiphany: he was in love again.

Chapter Eight

ABOMINABLE, BASE, CARNAL, VOLUPTUOUS

"[We] came to Glastonbury on Friday last. Went to the abbot, at Sharpham… As his answer was not to our purpose, advised him to call to mind what he had forgotten and tell the truth. [We] visited the abbey, searched his study, and found a book against the King's divorce from the lady Dowager, and divers pardons, copies of bulls, and the counterfeit life of Thos. Bequet in print… Examined him again on the articles received from Cromwell. His answers which we send will show his cankered and traitorous heart. And so… we have conveyed him from hence unto the Tower, being but a very weak man and sickly…"

Richard Pollard, Thomas Moyle, and Richard Layton, to Thomas Cromwell, September 1539, upon the dissolution of Glastonbury Abbey

Buried in Ambassador John Hutton's list of potential wives, there was something that might have given pause. "The duke of Cleves has a daughter but there is no great praise either of her personage or her beauty." It would have suited Thomas Cromwell to ignore this, but, given his workload, it would not be surprising if he overlooked it.

OPPOSITE: *Brilliant, ruthless, Machiavellian, complex, and contradictory, Thomas Cromwell was the chief architect of the Dissolution of the Monasteries. Holbein's portrait depicts a man of undoubted intelligence, brooding, cunning, unknowable.*

The correspondence that he dealt with as Chief Minister, the sheer quill-pushing, was staggering in its volume and import. From assizes across the realm came reports of crime and punishment, with casual references to gibbet and rack. The Tudor chronicler William Harrison wrote approvingly that "there is not one year commonly wherein three hundred or four hundred are not devoured and eaten up by the gallows."

It was open season for spies, informants, tattlers, and grudge-bearers: "Of late, certain persons have conceived mischievous letters…" "Certain malefactors in Oxford have customably eaten flesh this Lent…" "Divers persons have eaten flesh yesterday, being Ember Day…" "Concerning certain priests of Sarum…" "One John Adryan seems to favour as he dare, the Bishop of Rome." "Sir John Davy, curate of Radley, has spoken many traitorous words…" "The parson of Burfield has kept a concubine these 20 years…"

A rumor took hold that Henry was dead, no sooner scotched in one town than spreading in another. For repeating the gossip, a fuller named Edward Lyttelworke was sentenced to be "set on the pillory" on market day, his ears nailed shut and afterward cut off. He was roped to a cart horse, stripped naked, and whipped around the town.

Rebellions sprang up like brushfires, not just the Pilgrimage of Grace but spontaneous civil disorder. In January 1537 Sir Francis Bigod led an uprising in the far North. The rebels were intercepted by the Duke of Norfolk and 74 men were hanged on Carlisle's city walls. Henry wrote to the Duke that he should "cause such dreadful executions to be done upon a good number of the inhabitants of every town, village and hamlet that have offended, as they may be a fearful spectacle to all others." Norfolk duly obeyed.

By contrast, the indictment of the "Exeter Conspirators" was largely a Cromwell fabrication to eliminate remnants of the Plantagenet dynasty. The evidence rested on "certain proofs and confessions" extracted from a suicidal Sir Geoffrey Pole over months in the Tower. The Marquess of Exeter and Sir Edward Neville were beheaded for allegedly plotting to depose Henry in favor of Cardinal Reginald Pole, papal legate to the Low Countries. Since

the cardinal had evaded assassination and defied Henry's commands to come home to be decapitated, others had to pay.

Sir Nicholas Carew went to the block—after serving on the jury that indicted Exeter. Cromwell and Carew had schemed against Anne Boleyn. Now Cromwell turned on his old ally, producing incriminating letters.

Most odious was the imprisoning of Margaret Pole, Countess of Salisbury, Henry's mother's cousin, aged around 65, whose "crime" was to have been the mother of Cardinal Pole. Her eventual execution in 1541 would be effected by an inexperienced boy, hacking away blindly at her head and neck with an axe.

By 1538, nearly 30 years after Henry's coronation, when Heaven had smiled and Earth rejoiced and all was "milk and honey and nectar," the country had descended into a dystopian nightmare.

With all his commitments, Thomas Cromwell somehow found time to orchestrate the Dissolution of the Monasteries. The Act of Suppression of 1536 had targeted the smaller foundations. Now the greater religious houses would be turned over.

Hit squads were dispatched to obtain "surrenders." Almost every day came inventories from dissolved monasteries, nunneries, friaries, priories, and abbeys. Compliant monastery residents were pensioned off. If they would not surrender properties that were, anyway, not legally theirs, their buildings and contents, jewels, plate, lands, and livestock were seized. Understandably, most acquiesced "without constraint, coercion or compulsion."

In all, some eight hundred religious houses were closed, and eight thousand or so monks and nuns were displaced. The poor and infirm who had looked to the monasteries for succor must henceforth look elsewhere.

Churches and shrines were desecrated. Abbots who stood firm were hanged for constructive treason. So passed Richard Whiting of Glastonbury, Robert Hobbes of Woburn, Thomas Marshall of Colchester…

The destruction of historic buildings, monastic libraries, and ecclesiastical treasures was one of the most atrocious campaigns of vandalism England had ever known. Ruins littered the landscape. But the selling off and leasing of monastic properties was inspired. With a stake in so much real estate, a lot of people also had a stake in the Reformation.

Of course, the monasteries were ripe for reform. Corruption was endemic in a Church wallowing in money. Twenty-eight cartloads of jewels were borne away from Thomas Becket's shrine at Canterbury, and Becket was posthumously tried for "in his lifetime having disturbed the realm." His

BELOW: *The ruins of Glastonbury Abbey, dissolved in 1539. It was one of the richest prizes seized by the Crown in the Dissolution. In November the frail old abbot, Richard Whiting, was hanged, drawn, and quartered for "divers and sundry treasons," having been dragged through town on a hurdle.*

bones were dug up and burned, the treasures confiscated by the king. No one afterward was to call Becket "Saint." (Today the shrine of St Thomas Becket at Canterbury Cathedral is simple and moving.)

The human cost and pathos of the Dissolution can be best appreciated by perusing the inventories. From the buttery and kitchen at Austin Friars in Ludlow: "a little table, 2 trestles and a form, 2 old cupboards, a pan, kettle and other utensils." From the upper chamber at Whitefriars, Ludlow: "a bedstead, a table, 3 trestles and a form. An old stained cloth. A fair long coffer." From the warden's upper chamber at Greyfriars, Ipswich: "an old counter, a proper cupboard, the hangings poor, a pewter basin and ewer, 5 chairs, certain small images, an andiron and two pairs of tongs." Towels and tablecloths from the buttery. A pair of scales from the cheese house. Eighteen hangings "of small value" from the choir. One whole way of life obliterated.

On April 10, 1540, the last house, Waltham Abbey, founded by King Harold before the Norman Conquest, was surrendered. Thomas Cromwell had boasted that he would make Henry "the richest Prince in Christendom," and he was delivering on his promise. As a marriage broker he was less successful.

✒ Twelfth Night—or What You Will Not

In the Burrell Collection in Glasgow, Scotland, there is a carved bedhead adorned with the entwined monograms "H" and "A." An inscription declares this to be the bed of Henry King of England and France, Lord of Ireland, Defender of the Faith under God and Supreme Head of the Church of all England. On the king's side a male figure parts his doublet to reveal an oversized codpiece. On the queen's, a female figure holds in one hand a serpent, in the other an upturned sword. On the spandrel on the king's side hovers a priapic male sprite. On the queen's side a similarly lewd female disports herself.

The symbolism of fertility and virility were not, in the event, to work magic, nor to lend erotic charge to the wedding night. The upturned sword was wishful thinking. Fortunate Anne would be spared the pressure endured by her predecessors to conceive; there would be no question of a Duke of York from this marriage.

"How liked you the Queen?" asked an apprehensive Cromwell the next morning. "I liked her not before," gloomed Henry. "But now I like her much worse." He had left her, he said, "as good a maid as I had found her"—which, in his judgment, was not good at all. He had felt Anne's breasts and belly, and convinced himself that she was not a virgin. She was, he told Sir Anthony Denny, "not as she was reported."

The suggestion is risible. Anne was so naive that when, in June, one of her ladies, Jane Rochford, questioned her, Anne appeared unaware that her marriage had not been consummated. At night Henry would take her hand, kiss her, and bid her "goodnight, sweetheart"—wasn't that enough? If there was to be a royal baby, responded Lady Rochford, there would have to be more than that!

Jane Rochford, of all people, should not have been surprised by Henry's inadequacy. She had heard from her husband's sister, Anne Boleyn, that he had neither "vertu" nor "puissance"—neither skill nor virility. In testifying to this, indeed, she had helped to send both Anne and her own husband, George Boleyn, to their deaths.

Troubled by his inability to perform, Henry was characteristically keen to blame his young wife. Anne's body, he complained to his physicians, was "in such a sort disordered and indisposed" that she did not arouse him. The "hanging of her breasts and looseness of her flesh" discouraged him. He felt an overpowering "loathsomeness" (reluctance).

Despite his chagrin and resentment, Henry had by April raised Thomas Cromwell to Lord Great Chamberlain and Earl of Essex. The reason for his magnanimity is no mystery. He had fallen for one of Anne's maids, Kathryn Howard. According to her step-grandmother and guardian, the Dowager Duchess of Norfolk, he "did cast fantasy to her" at first sight.

Kathryn had none of the sophistication of her cousin, Anne Boleyn. She was born into straitened circumstances, to Lord Edmund Howard and his wife Joyce (Jocosa) Culpeper, in around 1523, when Anne was already at court and stealing hearts.

All that can be said of Kathryn's appearance is that she was petite, even tiny. A portrait in the National Portrait Gallery, once believed to be of her, is labeled "An unknown woman." It is "after Holbein," dates from the late

17th century, and depicts a woman in no way reminiscent of the flighty teenager who rekindled the king's libido.

Edmund Howard was an ineffectual, querulous man, "beaten by the world" as he lamented. He lacked the drive of his brother-in-law Thomas Boleyn, who had kept his head down through his son's and daughter's travails, and thereby kept it on. Joyce Culpeper was a widow with four children when she married Edmund, giving birth to six or seven more and dying when Kathryn was a little girl.

Kathryn was sent to grow up in the household of the Dowager Duchess of Norfolk, Agnes Howard, in Surrey and Lambeth, where she was sexualized at a young age. The Duchess was in her 60s, a court veteran and matriarch to various waifs and strays. In her way she was admirable, but she was no substitute for a loving mother.

Kathryn's first sexual adventure, in 1536, was with a music teacher named Henry Mannox, who gave her lessons in more than just the virginal, though they stopped short of full intercourse. She "suffered him to handle and

touch… the secret parts of her body," and, lonely child, may have been solaced by kisses and cuddles.

Her next intimacy, in 1538, was with Francis Dereham, a gentleman pensioner in Agnes Howard's Lambeth mansion. There may have been some form of secret betrothal, for the relationship was fully consummated. He had no presentiment, of course, when he used Kathryn "in such sort as a man doth use his wife many and sundry times," that the damsel he was pleasuring was a future Queen of England.

At night Dereham and a partner in crime, Edward Waldegrave, would come to the room Jane shared with another girl, Joan Bulmer. They would stay until dawn, as Francis and Kathryn "kissed and hung by their bellies as if they were two sparrows."

An anonymous tip-off from Mannox had alerted the Duchess to these goings-on and she was "much offended." So *she* knew that Kathryn was no maid. Jane Bulmer knew. Henry Mannox knew. Edward Waldegrave knew. And Henry VIII? He had *absolutely no idea*.

Despite his serial marriages and sundry affairs, the king seems to have had scant understanding of female sexuality. It is a rich irony that he took Kathryn to be a virgin, and the chaste Anne of Cleves to be otherwise.

At some point in the spring of 1540 he had bedded Kathryn, while Dereham was appointed as a secretary at Hampton Court. Now Henry resolved to wed her as soon as cunning minds had found the formula to annul his fourth marriage. The issue of an earlier promise to the Duke of Lorraine's son, having been swept under the carpet, was brought out into the light and dusted down. With the existence of that contract, the nonconsummation of the marriage, and the fact that Henry had entered into it under duress from Cromwell, the grounds for divorce were cobbled together.

In July the Queen was advised, through an interpreter, of her husband's intentions and was humbly accepting. Stephen Gardiner, Bishop of Winchester, reported, "Without alteration of countenance, she answered that she was 'content always with your Majesty'… All thing shall proceed well to your Highness' virtuous desire." On July 11 Anne put her consent in writing to Henry, "though the case must needs be hard and sorrowful," for the great love she "bears his most noble person." She implored the king to take her as one of his most humble servants, so she might still sometimes "have the fruition" of his presence. To pacify Duke William, she wrote to him that the king had adopted her as his sister and used her with more liberality than she or her brother could wish.

Anne of Cleves is widely portrayed as placid, sweet-natured, and dull, but maybe she was keenly astute. In agreeing to a divorce she earned Henry's gratitude, which he expressed in a huge settlement that included Hever Castle, Anne Boleyn's childhood home, which had come to him upon the death of Thomas Boleyn in March 1539.

In his elevated state of mind he was disposed to generosity, and found that, after all, he liked Anne of Cleves very well indeed.

🖋 No Other Wish but His

July 28, 1540. Mr Thomas Cromwell, heretofore condemned by Parliament, this morning was beheaded in the usual place for such executions. Grace was made to him upon the method of his death, for his condemnation was to a more painful and ignominious penalty.

Charles de Marillac, Castillon's replacement as French ambassador, must have wondered, as we do, how Henry could dispense with the man who had served him so ingeniously for a decade. Marillac had heard from the king a far-fetched story that Cromwell had planned to impose Lutheran doctrine by armed force, but would not have credited it. Inevitably, Cromwell had made many powerful enemies, just waiting to dance on his grave. The Duke of Norfolk, when he came to arrest him, took unseemly delight in ripping the commoner's St George medal from around Cromwell's neck. Cromwell was taken by barge to the Tower. By an Act of Attainder, the terms of which he had himself devised, he stood accused of high treason and heresy and was condemned without trial.

Henry being Henry, it would not be very long before he would be ruing Cromwell's demise, saying that "upon light pretexts, by false accusations," they made him put to death the most faithful servant he ever had.

On the day of the execution, however, the king had other things on his mind. At Oatlands Palace, built using materials from the dissolved Chertsey Abbey, he married Kathryn Howard. The bride took for her emblem the rose crowned, and for her motto "No Other Wish but His." She vowed to be "bonaire and buxom in bed and in board." Whose bed, she did not stipulate.

Anne, "the king's good sister," was granted precedence over all women except the new queen and the princesses. To all appearances she was reconciled to her new status. She was even acquiring a taste for fashion. Marillac noted in mid-August that "she is as joyous as ever, and wears new dresses every day; which argues either prudent dissimulation or stupid forgetfulness of what should so closely touch her heart." She was on amicable terms with both Mary and Elizabeth, her English was improving, and she was winning the nation's affections.

Just after New Year, 1541, 12 months after her new fiancé had sprung himself upon her in disguise, Anne arrived at Hampton Court with her entourage. Her New Year's gift to Henry was two horses with violet velvet trappings. Conveyed to Kathryn's presence, she insisted upon kneeling to address her. Henry entered, bowed to Anne, embraced and kissed her. And after supper, when Henry had gone to bed, Anne and Kathryn danced together. Before Anne left again for Richmond, Kathryn passed on to her a gift she had received from Henry of a ring and two small dogs.

Once again, there were at intervals two queens at court, but these were not the bitter rivals that Katharine of Aragon and Anne Boleyn had been. Were it not for Henry's deteriorating health, this would have been a halcyon interlude. He was making efforts to get in shape, rising before dawn, hearing Mass at seven o'clock, then riding until ten o'clock. But he had a suppurating ulcer on one leg, which caused his calf to swell and induced such fevers that there were fears. For 10–12 days in March he was confined to his chamber and would not have his wife see him in such a miserable condition. His "rose without a thorn" was thus left to find other amusements.

Whether then or later that spring, Kathryn embarked upon an affair with Thomas Culpeper, a member Henry's Privy Chamber and a distant relative of her mother's. He was a young man both handsome and (if this story be true) vile. Two years earlier, it was said, he had raped a park-keeper's wife while accomplices held her down. He had then murdered one of the villagers who tried to apprehend him. Henry, apprised of these crimes, had pardoned him. Boys will be boys.

Preparations were meanwhile under way for Henry's summer progress, which would take him to York and keep the court away until October. On

June 30 a far larger complement than usual went on the road. More than two hundred tents were carried, as artillery was dispatched to York by water. Such was Henry's fear of the mutinous North, he might have been going to war.

The enemy, however, turned out to be the weather. On July 18 the French ambassador, Marillac, wrote that it was cold and stormy, the rain incessant. Crops were flattened. Horses slipped and stumbled, strained in their traces, went down on their knees. Carts laden with tapestries and plate were mired in sludge. "Owing to some indisposition of the Queen and the weather not being yet settled, some say the journey is in terms of being broken," related Marillac. If it did go ahead, it would be thanks to the organizational skills of the Dukes of Norfolk and Suffolk.

There was, as ever, carnage all the way. Two or three hundred deer would be enclosed, and packs of greyhounds unleashed upon them. At Hatfield, in a single day, two hundred were slain, and the next day were taken "a great quantity of swans, two boats full of river birds, and as much of great pikes." And somehow also along the way, at Greenwich, Lincoln, and Pontefract, Kathryn and Culpeper sneaked off to hang together like sparrows.

On August 23, amid the blood fest, the sub-literate young queen sat down to write a letter. "Master Culpeper, I heartily recommend me unto you, praying you to send me word how that you do… It makes my heart die to think I cannot be always in your company. Come when my lady Rochforthe is here, for then I shall be best at leisure to be at your commandment… Yours as long as life endures."

York was another washout. Henry had extended an invitation to his nephew James V to meet with him there, but king, queen, and court waited in vain. The Scottish king had decided that this invitation from Uncle Henry was one he might well refuse.

It was a great and public humiliation for Henry, but nothing compared with what awaited him back in London.

✒ No more the time to dance

The progress was making its return when Archbishop Thomas Cranmer received a visit from John Lascelles, a sewer (server) in the king's Privy Chamber and former servant of Thomas Cromwell. The man had a tale to tell that made Cranmer's hair stand on end. His sister Mary had been a chambermaid to the Dowager Duchess Agnes and was one of dozens who had no illusions about Henry's "rose."

When Henry's weary cavalcade came clattering home, the Archbishop had the distressing task of telling him all he had learned. He chose not to speak of

it, but, on November 2, at Hampton Court, handed him a document detailing Lascelles's allegations. The revelations about Kathryn's past worked upon Henry most terribly. From initial disbelief he moved to weeping and seemed almost deranged. On November 5, he left Hampton Court suddenly after dinner, aboard his barge, leaving Kathryn to face the music.

Cranmer's next heavy duty was to interview the queen, "whose state it would have pitied any man's heart to see." He went two or three times to her chamber, but she was too distraught to make much sense. The line of questioning—first to overstate her crimes, then to assert the justice of the laws, and finally to "signify the king's mercy"—was contrived to break her down, but such was her frenzy that Cranmer weakened and began with the last. The promise of mercy undid her, for, she said, it made her offences seem the more heinous. And this before her adultery with Culpeper c ame to light.

Henry had showered his fifth wife with gifts of jewelry, but her chests and coffers were swiftly locked and placed under guard. She was removed to Syon House where she was "lodged moderately, as her life has deserved." Everyone and anyone was hauled in for interrogation. Henry Mannox swore that he and

Kathryn had been in love, but that the Duchess, finding them together one day, "gave Mrs Kathryn two or three blows" and ordered her never again to be alone with him. He then implicated Francis Dereham and Edward Waldegrave. Dereham confessed to having carnal knowledge of Kathryn—but only before her marriage.

One Margaret Morton disclosed how, at Hatfield, she saw the queen look out of her chamber window at Culpeper, "after such sort that she thought there was love between them." The queen had given orders that none of her ladies should enter her bedchamber unless called. At Luddington she had given Jane Rochford a sealed letter to deliver, with her apologies that she could not write better.

A Katherine Tylney said that, at Lincoln, "the Queen went two nights to Lady Rochford's chamber, which was up a little pair of stairs by the Queen's chamber." At 2 a.m. the queen was still not abed.

Jane Rochford was adamant that she had heard and seen nothing. She *thought* the Queen had known Culpeper carnally. One night at Lincoln, Kathryn had been at the back door waiting for him at 11 p.m. when a watchman came with a light and locked the door. Culpeper picked the lock and came in—but she, Lady Rochford, was asleep.

On November 11, Marillac wrote to King Francis of how Kathryn fared. "The way taken is the same as with Queen Anne who was beheaded; she has taken no pastimes but kept in her chamber, whereas, before, she did nothing but dance and rejoice, and now when the musicians come they are told that it is no more the time to dance."

On November 24, Kathryn, already stripped of her title, was indicted for leading "an abominable, base, carnal, voluptuous and vicious life," while maintaining the appearance of chastity and honesty.

The Tower of London was overflowing with Howards, step-Howards, and "light young men… privy to the naughtiness of the Queen and Dereham." Among them were Lord William Howard, his wife, Margaret, and his sister the Countess of Bridgewater. Their crime was "misprision of treason"—of having foreknowledge that someone meant to commit treason. Even the protesting Dowager Duchess Agnes was hauled in.

The craven Thomas Howard, 3rd Duke of Norfolk, wrote to Henry to distance himself from "mine ungracious mother-in-law [stepmother], mine unhappy brother and his wife, with my lewd sister of Brydgewater." He was sure that their being taken to the Tower "was not done but for some false proceedings against your Majesty." He begged assurance of the king's favor, without which he could not bear to live.

On December 10, Dereham was hanged, drawn, and quartered, though no adultery had been proved. Culpeper was beheaded. Even under torture he had denied that sexual intercourse had taken place, and was condemned only for intent to commit adultery.

Another Christmas, another New Year came and went, with no one in the mood for "disguisings." On February 10, 1542, Kathryn, dressed in black velvet, was bundled, struggling, aboard a small, covered barge and borne away to her prison.

Like the men who died for loving her, she had never confessed to adultery. In a final act of pettiness, Henry sent some of his Privy Councillors to her, to get back a ring worth only three gold crowns "unless the stone, as it is said, has some virtue against spasms," wrote Eustace Chapuys.

That Sunday Kathryn Howard was told to prepare for death, and she made a strange request. Could they bring the block to her so she might "know how to place herself"? It was brought to her so she might "make trial of it."

They came for her at 7 a.m., when Henry would have been at Mass. She was almost beyond speech, but managed to stammer a few words, saying that she deserved to die a thousand deaths for offending the king who had been so good to her. She laid her head upon the block, as her cousin Anne had done, and as Jane Rochford would do after her. Their headless bodies joined those of Jane's husband and her sister-in-law in the Chapel of St Peter ad Vincula at the Tower.

Anne Boleyn was a clever, educated, worldly and beguiling woman innocent of the charges brought against her. Kathryn was a childish, feckless, impressionable, vulnerable girl, perhaps still in her teens, almost certainly guilty of adultery, and yet, to the last, an innocent.

"The common voice," wrote Marillac, "is that this King will not be long without a wife, for the great desire he has to have further issue." It would not, though, prove to be so easy.

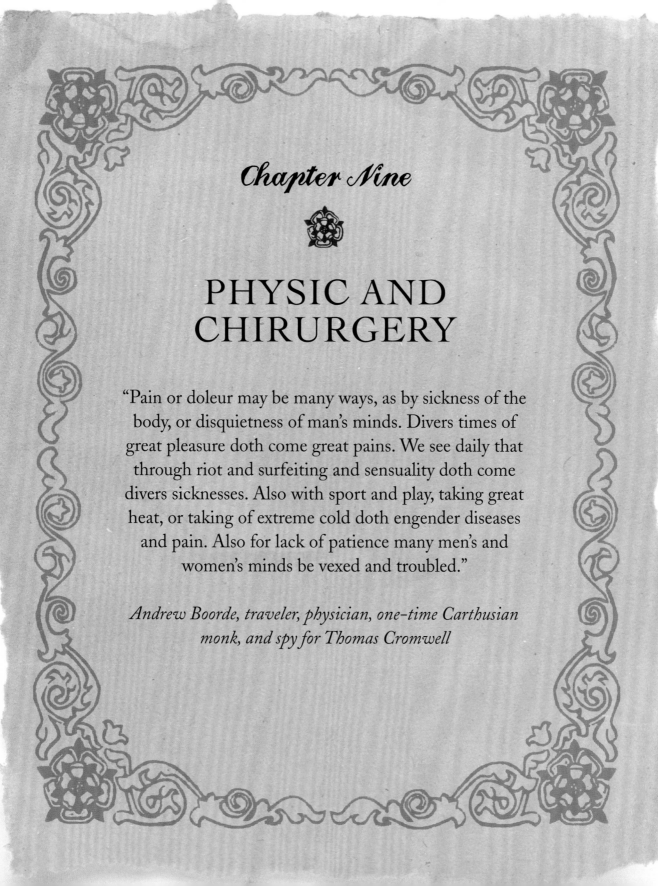

Chapter Nine

PHYSIC AND CHIRURGERY

"Pain or doleur may be many ways, as by sickness of the body, or disquietness of man's minds. Divers times of great pleasure doth come great pains. We see daily that through riot and surfeiting and sensuality doth come divers sicknesses. Also with sport and play, taking great heat, or taking of extreme cold doth engender diseases and pain. Also for lack of patience many men's and women's minds be vexed and troubled."

Andrew Boorde, traveler, physician, one-time Carthusian monk, and spy for Thomas Cromwell

"February 25, 1542. The King has been in better spirits since the execution, and during the last three days before Lent there has been much feasting… Unless Parliament prays him to take another wife, he will not, I think, be in a hurry to marry; besides, few, if any, ladies now in court would aspire to such an honor."

Droll Eustace Chapuys was not actually referring to Henry's desirability, but to a stringent new law. Henceforth, if the king wished to marry, the lady would be bound, on pain of death, to declare if charges of misconduct could be brought against her. Anyone who even suspected impropriety and failed to reveal it faced life imprisonment.

Henry had never been less eligible. His physical, mental, and moral degeneration must have been obvious to all. His contrariety and irascibility may have owed something to alcohol. As the French ambassador, Charles de Marillac, had noted, "He is very stout and marvelously excessive in drinking and eating, so that people worth credit say he is often of a different opinion in the morning than after dinner."

He was also, if not a hypochondriac, at least morbidly preoccupied with illness. He had no knowledge of germs but he apperceived the dangers of a cough or sneeze. The impeachment of Cardinal Wolsey had included a charge that he, "knowing himself to have the foul and contagious disease of the great pox [syphilis], broken out upon him in divers places of his body, came daily to your Grace… blowing upon your most noble Grace with his perilous and infective breath, to the marvellous danger of your highness."

Henry's particular horror was the sweating sickness, or *Sudor Anglicus*. At the first rumor of it he would take himself miles from court and capital. This "baleful affliction" was perhaps a strain of influenza and manifested like a curse visited upon Tudor males (a judgment from God, some thought, for usurping the throne). As lethal as an arrow, it was at work on the field of Bosworth in 1485 when Henry Tudor seized the crown. There were four outbreaks, the most virulent in 1528, and the last in 1551 during the reign of Edward VI, after which it disappeared for ever. In his Brevyary of Helthe the 16th-century physician Andrew Boorde advised keeping the patient in bed, entirely covered but for the face, with a fire in the room, with no food, but with ale and warm drinks sucked through a swan's or goose's quill. The patient should also choke down a sapphire, or hold it in his hand.

Henry was spared the sweating sickness, but in March 1514, as he prepared to invade France, he was struck down with a fever said to have been smallpox, caused by "a corruption of the blood." He had also at one time contracted malaria from the mal air.

Belief in miasmas, the four humors, and astrology were central tenets of the medical orthodoxy of the day. Humorism, which had its roots in ancient Greece, holds that four liquids within the human body—blood, phlegm, yellow bile, and black bile—must be kept in balance for the health of body and mind.

If Henry was "ill-humored" it was not to be wondered at. He was frequently in excruciating pain. He had been prone to migraines since a jousting accident in 1528, when he failed to close his visor and was rammed in the brow by the Duke of Suffolk's lance. Three years earlier, he had been out hawking when he fell from his horse into a ditch, and was saved from drowning by a footman, Edmund Moody, who raised his head out of the water. In 1527 he hurt his foot when playing tennis; the black velvet slipper that he wore became a fashion item.

In January 1536 he had had a second, near-fatal accident in the tiltyard, when, wrote Chapuys, "the King being mounted on a great horse to run at the lists, both fell so heavily that everyone thought it a miracle he was not killed, but he sustained no injury." In fact, he was unconscious for two hours and very possibly suffered brain damage—as well as (she believed) causing Anne Boleyn to miscarry.

The varicose leg ulcers that bedeviled him may have been the result of vanity. As he had boasted to the Venetian envoy Sebastian Giustiniani, he had "a very good calf," and wore constricting garters to accentuate the muscle.

In May 1538, while Hans Holbein was at large in Europe capturing the likenesses of nubile duchesses, the French ambassador Castillon wrote, "This King has had stopped one of the fistulas of his legs, and for 10 or 12 days the humors which had no outlet were like to have stifled him, so that he was sometime without speaking, black in the face, and in great danger." Medical historians speculate that he suffered a pulmonary embolism. From that day his physicians ensured that the ulcers were never closed.

Syphilis has been posited as a reason why Henry's wives suffered so many miscarriages and stillbirths. His mood swings, lapses of judgment, and incandescent rages are said to have been symptomatic of it. One suspects an element of moral judgment—a sense that, if Henry didn't have venereal disease, he ought to have done—since the syphilis argument defies reason. Henry manifested none of the most obvious physical symptoms of the disease

ABOVE: *Working from
earlier sketches of the irascible
king, Holbein painted*
**Henry VIII and the Barber
Surgeons** *in 1543 to mark
the merger of the Guild of
Surgeons and Company of
Barbers. In the painting,
which was badly damaged in
the Great Fire of London in
1666 and which has
additions by other artists,
Henry hands a royal charter
to his sergeant-surgeon,
Thomas Vicary. His personal
physicians are on the left of
the picture. The tight garter
on his left leg may have
caused health problems (see
also pages 174–5).*

or of mercury poisoning from the "cure." (Spend a night with Venus and
a lifetime with Mercury, ran the joke.) Had he done so, we can be sure we
would have heard about it from the likes of Eustace Chapuys.

Another factor is that Henry's children displayed no signs of congenital
syphilis, such as "saddle nose," peg teeth, clouded corneas, blindness, poor
hearing, or joint swelling. Edward was frail and Mary was small like her
mother, but Elizabeth lived to her 70th year and reigned for 45 years. All were
bright and precocious learners.

In fact, Henry's behavior in his declining years was entirely consistent with
his sense of having been double-crossed by Fate, and failed and deceived by
his women and advisors. Here was a man who had divorced two wives,
ordered the execution of two others, and been robbed of another in her
childbed. He had rid himself of the devout Thomas More, and of such
assiduous servants as Wolsey and Cromwell. If Henry's conscience did not
trouble him, it was because he took refuge in reproaching others. Repression,
denial, projection, displacement—the whole box of tricks.

His unstable temperament was further associated with his catastrophic
loss of fitness. He had developed a noticeable limp and by 1543 would have
resort to "walking staves." Deprived of his beloved sports and piling on the

ABOVE: *Albrecht Dürer's woodcut of a man afflicted with syphilis. Imported from the New World as part of the "Columbian exchange," the disease was seen as God's punishment for blasphemy, but was also attributed to the malign conjunction of the planets.*

pounds, he was caught in a vicious cycle, as depression caused him to binge on food and drink. Diabetes, or "immoderate pyssinge," is another likely suspect in causing his emotional instability.

The greatest bane of Henry's life was his failure to father numerous male heirs and spares—or, rather, his wives' failure to present him with them. Setting aside the syphilis canard, it is worth considering more recent conjecture. If Henry's blood carried the so-called "Kell" antigen, and if his wives were Kell-negative, this could explain their miscarriages. When a Kell-negative woman conceives a first child with a Kell-positive man, she may be delivered of a healthy Kell-positive baby, but antibodies produced in a subsequent pregnancy will attack a Kell-positive fetus.

Since Mary was born of a fifth pregnancy, she is assumed to have inherited Henry's recessive Kell gene. Anne Boleyn, having given birth to Elizabeth, had but a 50-50 chance of bearing another healthy child. Then again, horseback riding, obesity, alcohol abuse, and hot clothing can all impair male fertility.

McLeod syndrome, a recessive mutation of the Kell blood group, could have caused Henry's apparent psychosis, and supporters of the Kell/McLeod hypothesis maintain that it was this that transformed him in middle age from a fun-loving, affectionate prince to a barbarous despot. Others cite the jousting accident of 1536 as the point at which he "changed." But did he?

Henry was just eight, a pint-sized Duke of York, when Erasmus first met him and noted "a certain royal demeanor"—imperiousness and presumption were already in his makeup. He ascended the throne with the aim of invading France and restating England's claim to the French crown. The execution of his father's men Empson and Dudley was merely first blood. He was vain and self-indulgent, demanding his own way in all things. Even those famed masques in the "fun times" were assertions of male hierarchy and kingly power. One sees not overnight change but a gradual, ineluctable slide into depravity. Power tends to corrupt—and absolute power corrupts absolutely.

But poor Henry! Who knows? Maybe he was right. Maybe really nothing was his own fault after all.

✒ In sickness and in health

On 12 July 1543, in an upper oratory called "the Quynes Pryevey closet" within the honor of Hampton Court… in presence of the noble gentle persons named at the foot of this instrument… the King and Lady Katherine Latymer alias Parr being met there for the purpose of solemnising matrimony between them, Stephen bp. of Winchester proclaimed… that they were met to join in marriage the said King and Lady Katherine…

After Kathryn Howard, as Chapuys had surmised, Henry had not been in haste to marry again, and courtiers were too unnerved to push a niece or sister his way lest some skeleton come clattering out of the closet.

One woman, however, would have been happy to step into the breach. At Richmond, Anne of Cleves had received the news of her successor's arrest with a little surge of triumph. Her English ladies were thrilled. Jane Batsey and Elizabeth Basset had to be hauled before the Council for exulting "What? Is God working his own work to make Lady Anne of Cleves queen again?" Batsey had added, "It is impossible that so sweet a Queen as Anne could be so utterly put down," to which Basset had replied, "What a man the king is! How many wives will he have?" A terrified Basset had pleaded that shock at the tidings of Kathryn's naughty behavior had caused her momentarily to lose her mind.

Two days later, the Council, which was then considering the accusations against Kathryn, had also to investigate "a new matter, being a report that the Lady Anne of Cleves should be delivered of a fair boy and whose should it be but the King's majesty?"

It was a fortnight before this was dismissed as "an abominable slander," whereupon her brother, the Duke of Cleves, began pressing vainly for a reconciliation with Anne. What was done, came the stern reply, had been done for good reason, whatever the world might think.

Still, Anne continued to nurture hope of a rethink. When, not quite 18 months after Kathryn's execution, Henry married Katherine Parr, Chapuys wrote of Anne "having especially taken great grief and despair at the king's espousal of this last wife, who is not nearly so beautiful as she, besides that there is no hope of issue, seeing that she had none with her two former husbands."

Katherine Parr was a fascinating woman. If she had been Henry's first wife, and not "this last," she would attract far more attention today. She was born in

ABOVE: *Sudeley Castle in Gloucestershire was the property of Jane Seymour's foolhardy brother Thomas, who had designs on Princess Elizabeth—before making another prestigious royal marriage. "He spared no cost his lady to delight."*

around 1512, one of three children of Sir Thomas Parr of Kendal in Westmorland, and Maud Greene. Sir Thomas, who had been a companion-in-arms to Henry upon his coronation, died in 1517. Maud, a former lady-in-waiting to Katharine of Aragon, needed her children to marry well.

At 17, Katherine wed Sir Edward Borough, son of Anne Boleyn's Lord Chamberlain, Lord Burgh. The year after Sir Edward's death in 1533, she took a second, much older husband, John Neville, 3rd Baron Latimer, of Snape Castle in Yorkshire. Latimer was a widower twice over, with a son, John, and daughter, Margaret.

In common with that other great northern dynasty the Percys, the Nevilles were continually in the thick of history. Whenever there was Northern insurrection, there was usually a Neville and a Percy in the mix somewhere. However, Lord Latimer's involvement in the uprising known as the Pilgrimage of Grace had been a case of coercion by the insurgents' leader, Robert Aske. When, in 1537, Latimer was required to travel south in order to explain himself to the king, Katherine and her stepdaughter, Margaret, aged 11 or 12, were placed under house arrest by rebels to secure his return.

Katherine's grace under pressure, her experience of running a household, and the affection she inspired in her stepchildren would be hallmarks of her marriage to Henry.

In his dying days Latimer was an invalid requiring nursing and Katherine spent more time in her London home. She had fallen in love with Thomas Seymour, and imagined marrying him when she came into the Neville fortune—but then Seymour's brother-in-law claimed her. The marriage that her heart desired would have to be deferred until after Henry's death, when she was to write to Thomas in her elegant hand that "as truly as God is God, my mind was fully bent the other time I was at liberty to marry you before any man I knew." At Henry's behest she "renounced utterly" her own will. In this context, her queenly motto, "To Be Useful in All I Do," may be read with a long-suffering sigh.

Katherine's widowhood was a blessing, for, unlike Kathryn Howard, she could not be presumed to be a virgin. If there had been intimacy with Seymour, both were shrewd enough to conceal it. In any case, Henry was no longer avid for sex and issue, though hope remained of more princes. What he needed was a nursemaid. And for all his reputation as a playboy of the Western world, his greatest lust had always been for action on the battlefield—in France.

Since his nephew James V of Scotland had refused to repudiate the Auld Alliance with the enemy, France, the way was open for a Gallic invasion of England from the north. Henry was determined to impose his suzerainty upon his Catholic neighbor. A battle at Solway Moss in the Borders in 1542 had resulted in the massacre of hundreds of fleeing Scotsmen and the taking of 1,200 prisoners. Though the Scots outnumbered the English by six-to-one, there was but a handful of English casualties.

The devastated James V died two weeks later, a few days after the birth of his daughter to Mary of Guise (the Madame de Longueville whom Henry had craved to marry). Thus, within her first week of life, the infant became Mary, Queen of Scots.

On July 1, 1543, a treaty was signed with Scotland, decreeing that Prince Edward, now six, would marry Mary. When she turned 11 she was to be delivered into the hands of English commissioners at Berwick, a contract of marriage having been made by proxy. When the Scottish Parliament repudiated the treaty, Henry was fit to be tied.

KATHARINE PARRE

☙ The manner of the wooing

Put all to fire and sword, burn Edinburgh town, so razed and defaced when you have sacked and gotten what ye can of it, as there may remain forever a perpetual memory of the vengeance of God lightened upon [them] for their falsehood and disloyalty… Put man, woman and child to fire and sword without exception, where any resistance shall be made against you.

With these orders from Henry, there began a long and deeply shaming episode in English history. English soldiers, led by the Earl of Hertford (Henry's other Seymour brother-in-law, Edward), murdered, raped, and torched their way across the south of Scotland. In Edinburgh, Holyrood House and Abbey were devoured by flames.

ABOVE: *Twice widowed and aged 31 when she married Henry, Katherine Parr is a model of composure in this portrait, which hangs at Montacute House in Somerset. By an unknown artist, it dates from about two years after her marriage to Henry. London's National Portrait Gallery holds a second painting of her, which was once thought to depict Lady Jane Grey.*

Melrose Abbey was reduced to ruins. The people of Dunbar were burned alive in their beds.

This campaign to force Scotland into an alliance with England, launched by Henry VIII and still being waged after his death, was later christened the Rough Wooing. "We liked not the manner of the wooing," George Gordon, 4th Earl of Huntly, had said, "and we could not stoop to being bullied into love."

At the age of five, Mary was sent to France, where she would wed the Dauphin, returning, widowed, at 18 to give Queen Elizabeth problems and to set the Nevilles and Percys off again.

So this was the king that Katherine Parr had vowed to have and to hold, in sickness and in health. She was a tranquil presence, balm to the king's family, who were now more often brought together and for whom she showed genuine care, as she had for her stepdaughter, Margaret Neville. Eustace Chapuys, who had worried so deeply for Mary, could finally relax.

Katherine adored her parrots and greyhounds and enjoyed dressing up in silks and dancing—she was fun-loving and stylish. But when Henry was ailing she would sleep in a small room off his bedchamber, and she would take his sore leg upon her knee.

In July 1544, with Scotland grimly holding out against the English, Henry encased his broken, bloated body in his king-sized armor, was winched up onto his poor horse, and went off to lay siege to Boulogne. By 1539–40 his waist had measured 52 inches (132cm), up from 35 inches (90cm) in 1515, and by 1547 he was close to 390 pounds (almost 28 stone, or 178kg). Chapuys wrote to Charles V:

> *Many of those who are about the king's person do not wish him to cross the Channel. They are afraid of his suddenly failing in ill health, and also that, if they have to take care of his person, all military operations will necessarily be delayed and the march of their army slackened; besides which the king's chronic disease and great obesity require particular care lest his life should be endangered.*

However, vanity dictated that Henry lead his troops. He was tremendously bucked up by the whole thing, though his armor had to be cut away to relieve the swelling of his leg.

The country was meanwhile left in the safe hands of his regent, Queen Katherine, playing Penelope to her gargantuan Odysseus. She waved her warrior husband off at Dover and wrote him tender, yearning letters, saying "the want of your presence, so much desired and beloved by me, maketh me that I cannot quietly pleasure in anything until I hear from your majesty… And whereas I know your majesty's absence is never without great need, yet love and affection compel me to desire your presence." God, the knower of secrets, could judge the truth of her words, not only written in ink but impressed on her heart.

She may have been sincere, but she had a rare and special gift for cajoling and dissembling, to manage Henry and his megrims. In 1545 it was this that was to save her life.

Divorced, beheaded, died, divorced, beheaded… beheaded? It could have come to that. Another extraordinary thing about Katherine was her authorship. Traumatized by the Pilgrimage of Grace, she had become a Reformist, increasingly convinced and confident in her views. Her *Prayers or Meditations*, known as *The Queen's Prayers*, went through numerous editions without raising eyebrows. Her autobiographical *Lamentation or Complaint of a*

ABOVE: *The armor in which Henry carapaced his corpulent frame in later life. Thought to have been made by a Milanese merchant, and designed for use on foot and on horseback, it may have been worn at the siege of Boulogne in 1544, during his last military campaign.*

Sinner, describing her struggle to find faith, was a more dangerous enterprise that would not see publication until Elizabeth's Protestant reign. In it she argued against denying the laity the right to read the Bible on the ground that they would "therefore fall into heresies." The King's Book, implemented in 1543, had banned poorer men and all but the wealthiest women from reading the scriptures. She was flying in the face of Henry's policy.

This was a perilous time for evangelists. The wind had changed—the weather vane had swung back toward Catholicism. Archbishop Cranmer was fortunate to survive the "Prebendaries' Plot" of April 1543, organized by Stephen Gardiner, Bishop of Winchester, and aimed at removing him from office to be burned at the stake. Henry, whose religious beliefs were as inconsistent as his moods, ignored the charges laid before him until July, when he simply told Cranmer to investigate them himself. Cranmer's martyrdom would have to wait for Mary's reign.

By 1546 the reactionaries Gardiner and the Duke of Norfolk were conspiring to expose Katherine's heresies. She liked to discuss religion with Henry and she misjudged how far she could push him. On one of his bad days in January, after she had left the room, he snarled, "A good hearing it is when women become such clerks, and a thing much to my comfort, to come in mine old days to be taught by my wife!"

In May, Katherine had her book collection smuggled from the palace. She ordered new coffers with locks.

In July, Bishop Gardiner told Henry that he would "disclose such treasons, cloaked with this cloak of heresy." His Majesty was "cherishing a serpent within his own bosom." Gardiner planned her arrest, but Katherine was handed a document detailing the charges to be brought against her. She at once ordered her ladies to destroy any incriminating books and went to see the king, making an impassioned speech about a wife's duty to submit to her husband, for her opinions were inferior to the superior wisdom of her lord. With a stroke of brilliance, she insisted that she argued with the king only to distract him from his pain. "And it is even so, sweetheart?" he smiled indulgently. "Then, perfect friends we are now again, as ever any time heretofore."

Contrary to her nursemaid image, then, Katherine Parr was a woman of considerable wiles. Soon after Henry's death, when she would have been officially in mourning, she wrote to Thomas Seymour, bidding him to Chelsea Manor for a tryst. "When it shall be your pleasure to repair hither you should take some pain to be early in the morning, that you may be gone again by seven o'clock, and so I suppose you may come without suspect."

RIGHT: *So bizarre was the appearance of this horned, bespectacled helmet that it was assumed to have belonged to Henry's favorite Fool, Will Somers. Made by Konrad Seusenhofer, for use in tournaments not battle, it was a gift to Henry from the Holy Roman Emperor Maximilian I in 1514. The spectacles were probably for appearance only, to exaggerate the grotesque effect, although we know from the inventory of Henry's possessions that he owned many jeweled eye glasses and spectacle cases.*

WILL, SUMMERS'S ARMOUR

...s preserved in the tower of London...

...ut as the Act directs by I.Herbert, Pall Mall. 1 June 1794.

ÆTATIS ·   SVE · 88 ·

ABOVE: *As one of Henry's personal physicians, John Chambers tended him throughout his reign—and his father before him. With his colleague Dr Butts, Chambers was instrumental in securing the king's divorce from Anne of Cleves, testifying that the marriage was not consummated.*

There is not a shred of evidence against her, but it would be amusing to think that Katherine Parr had committed adultery with her former fiancé and future husband—the one wife of Henry VIII to cuckold her husband and get away with it.

☙ Till death us do part

One important aspect of Henry's obsession with health was the influence it had on the practice of "physic." When he ascended the throne, England was lagging behind continental Europe in medicine. Physicians were poorly trained and unregulated; their practices were mired in superstition. All this would change during Henry's reign. It was he who endowed the first medical chairs in the country, the Regius Professorships at Oxford and Cambridge.

His interest was not purely personal but academic. He had genuine intellectual curiosity, and among the afternoon amusements at court was "the consecration and distribution of cramp-rings, or the inventing of plasters and compounds of medicine, an occupation in which the King took unusual pleasure." A remedy that Henry himself devised was "the gray plaster," an ointment to relieve inflammation and pain and to heal ulcers. It included such ingredients as rosebuds, honeysuckle leaves, violets, the suet of capons or hens, rose water, and white wine. He sent the Lord Mayor of London a recipe for a remedy against the plague: a mix of herbs, elder, briar leaves, ginger, and white wine. Taken for nine days, it would afford a year's protection, although should a "botch" appear within the nine days, the sufferer was to mix the remedy with mustard seed and apply it to the skin. The king also possessed medical texts, including the *Practica in Arte Chirurgica Compendiosa*, Giovanni da Vigo's seminal work on surgery.

The Physicians and Surgeons Act of 1511 decreed that physicians in London must graduate from Oxford or Cambridge, or be examined by the Bishop of London or the Dean of St Paul's Cathedral. In the provinces, practitioners would be examined by the bishop in their diocese.

In 1518, England's oldest medical college, the King's College of Physicians (the Royal College of Physicians), was founded by royal charter in London, at

ABOVE: *Another of Henry's trusted physicians, Sir William Butts knew how to calm and mollify the volatile king. Henry's failure to consummate his marriage to Anne of Cleves, Butts assured him, was of course not the result of his impotence but of her failure to excite him. He attended Henry to the last.*

the urging of Thomas Linacre, a humanist scholar and Henry's Royal Physician. The charter decreed that it should "curb the audacity of those wicked men who shall profess medicine more for the sake of their avarice than from the assurance of good conscience, whereby many inconveniences may ensue to the rude and credulous populace."

There was indeed a lot of quackery out there along with folk wisdom and plant lore. Apothecaries, the early pharmacists, grew herbs in physic gardens. As the monasteries had done, the great households and palaces had gardens for medicinal herbs.

As well as his physicians—Linacre, John Chambers, William Butts, George Owen—Henry appointed Thomas Vicary as Sergeant-Surgeon to the King in 1536. Four years later, Vicary incorporated barbers and surgeons into one company. A charter granted by Edward IV had allowed barbers to let blood, pull teeth, and perform minor operations, "exercising the Mystery of Art of Surgery." The new company implemented systematic teaching for all practitioners of "chirurgery." Vicary went on to write *A Tresure for English-Men Concerning the Anatomie of Man's Body*—the first English-language textbook on the subject.

Hans Holbein was commissioned to make a large painting commemorating the grant of the royal charter to the Company of Barbers and Guild of Surgeons. Henry did not sit for it, and Holbein, drawing upon earlier sketches, presented him as an iconic rather than a living figure, handing Vicary the charter. From now on, barbers would be limited to cutting hair, shaving, pulling teeth, and blood-letting. Surgeons alone could cut into bodies, and the company was granted, for dissection purposes, four bodies of executed criminals a year. Under Henry these were not in short supply.

In the last days of his life Henry was bedridden in a chamber reeking of pus. The doctors could do no more for him. Who was to tell him that his hour was nigh? The Treason Act, which Henry enacted, had made it a crime to speak of the king's death.

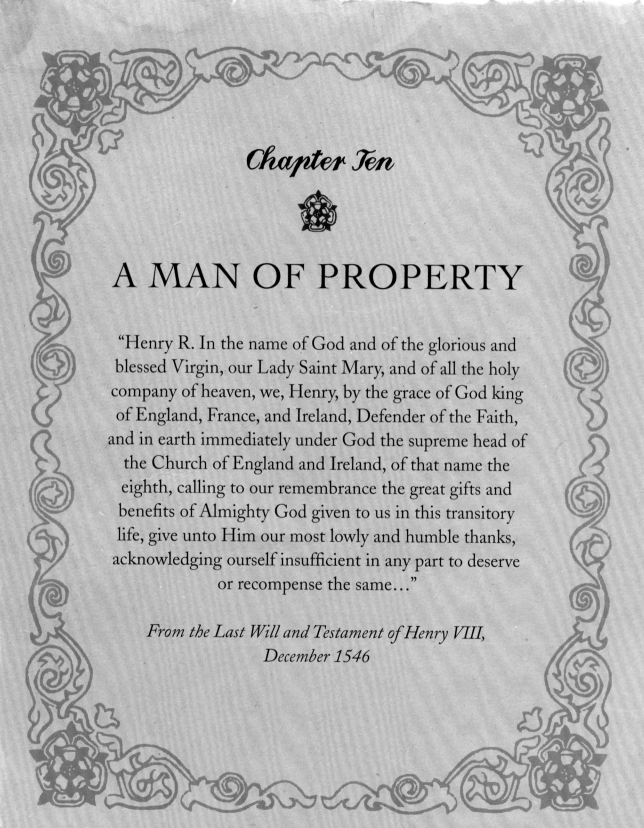

Chapter Ten

A MAN OF PROPERTY

"Henry R. In the name of God and of the glorious and blessed Virgin, our Lady Saint Mary, and of all the holy company of heaven, we, Henry, by the grace of God king of England, France, and Ireland, Defender of the Faith, and in earth immediately under God the supreme head of the Church of England and Ireland, of that name the eighth, calling to our remembrance the great gifts and benefits of Almighty God given to us in this transitory life, give unto Him our most lowly and humble thanks, acknowledging ourself insufficient in any part to deserve or recompense the same…"

From the Last Will and Testament of Henry VIII,
December 1546

Queen Katherine was not with her husband at his passing in his Privy Chamber in the small hours of January 28, 1547. Summoned to his deathbed, Thomas Cranmer asked the king for a sign that he could hear him, and Henry squeezed his hand. He was 55 and had reigned for nearly 38 years.

When Henry came to the throne, the coffers had been overflowing. The Dissolution of the Monasteries had enormously enriched him. He had spent the lot on making war, building the Navy Royal and creating Fortress Britain.

Always a passionate collector, he was the owner of some 70 palaces, stately homes, mansions, and hunting lodges, for many of which he had no earthly use, allowing some to disintegrate or be demolished.

Gone is Henry VII's Richmond Palace, home to the divorced Anne of Cleves; gone is Greenwich Palace, also known as the Palace of Placentia, scene of so many feasts and masques. The London palaces of Whitehall, Bridewell, and Baynards Castle have vanished, as has Henry VIII's Nonsuch Palace in Surrey, intended to outshine the Palace of Fontainebleau, which had been transformed in the Renaissance manner by his *bête noir* Francis I. Begun in 1538 and uncompleted at his death, Nonsuch Palace soaked up more than £25,000 in seven years. It was destroyed in the late 1600s when the Duchess of Cleveland, a mistress of Charles II, demolished it and sold the materials to pay gambling debts.

BELOW: *Begun in April 1538, Nonsuch Palace near Epsom in Surrey was built on the site of the razed village of Cuddington, cleared for the purpose of building the most fabulous palace the world had ever seen. It cost around £130 million in today's money and was still unfinished at the time of Henry's death.*

ABOVE: *Time and tide wait for no man, but with the astronomical clock created for him at Hampton Court by the French clockmaker Nicholas Oursian, Henry could keep track of both. It recorded the hour, day, month, high and low tides at London Bridge, and much more.*

Cardinal Wolsey's Hampton Court, although much altered for William and Mary after 1689, retains a good part of its 16th-century character, including the restored, industrial-scale kitchens. The astronomical clock, made for Henry by the French clockmaker Nicholas Oursian, was a marvel of its age.

Hampton Court has ghosts, of course. Kathryn Howard's shrieks are heard in the gallery through which they dragged her. People tell of seeing Anne Boleyn dressed in blue, walking slowly, sadly—and of Jane Seymour in both the Clock Court and Silver Stick Gallery.

In the crypt of the chapel of St Peter ad Vincula at the Tower of London, the bones of Anne Boleyn and Kathryn Howard keep cold company with the headless remains of George Boleyn, Sir Thomas More, John Fisher, Thomas Cromwell, and Lady Jane Grey, "the Nine-Day Queen" who so briefly succeeded Edward VI. There are many reported sightings of the shade of Anne, headless and otherwise, around the Tower.

At the Tudor redbrick St James's Palace, begun by Henry in 1531, a gatehouse bears his cipher, "HR." Here Anne Boleyn stayed after her coronation, and Henry FitzRoy, the King's illegitimate son, died aged 17. Windsor Castle, with its deer park, remains a prominent royal residence and a visitor attraction. At Eltham Palace, where Erasmus first met the lordly young Prince Henry, the Great Hall survives with its huge hammerbeam roof, within a 1930s Art Deco extravaganza.

In Kent, Hever Castle, Anne Boleyn's childhood home, granted to Anne of Cleves upon her divorce, retains a wonderful collection of Tudor portraits. Nearby is Penshurst Place, the fortified medieval manor forfeited to Henry on the attainder of the 3rd Duke of Buckingham. Beautiful, moated Leeds Castle, transformed into a palace for Katharine of Aragon, is the recreation of a medieval original, which fell into decay in the 1600s. Not very far distant is Knole House, which Henry demanded of Thomas Cranmer, much as he demanded Hampton Court of Wolsey.

In Lewes, Sussex, stands the timber-framed Anne of Cleves House, a small part of Anne's divorce settlement, with period furnishings, and traditional Tudor plantings in the gardens. Anne outlived Katherine Parr by nine years, residing in Chelsea Old Manor, where the recently widowed Katherine had kept her tryst with Thomas Seymour. Anne of Cleves died there on July 16, 1557, aged 41, and is entombed in Westminster Abbey, the only one of Henry's wives to be buried there. Kind and thoughtful to the last, she left money to her servants and asked in her will that Mary and Elizabeth reemploy them.

In Shropshire we may see the remains of Ludlow Castle, where Prince Arthur, heir to the throne, and his Spanish bride Katharine of Aragon fell ill and Arthur died.

Kimbolton Castle, Cambridgeshire, where Katharine of Aragon lived out her life as a divorcee, is today a school. Katharine's tomb in Peterborough Cathedral, Cambridgeshire, accords her a dignity that Henry denied her. He did not attend her funeral, and forbade Mary to do so.

BELOW: *Anne of Cleves House in Lewes, East Sussex, part of her divorce settlement, is a Tudor time capsule. It was part of Anne of Cleves's divorce settlement, although she never actually visited the humble dwelling. The bedroom and kitchen are furnished as they would have been at the time.*

ABOVE: *Elizabeth could have had no memory of her mother, Anne Boleyn. She loved her father, but her true feelings about Anne's execution are unknown. The fact that she commissioned this locket ring bearing their twin images suggests she felt an abiding loyalty to the woman she knew only from others' reports.*

Sudeley Castle in Gloucestershire, a Cotswolds limestone jewel, was granted by the new boy king, Edward VI, to his uncle Thomas Seymour. As Baron of Sudeley, Thomas brought his bride, Katherine, here. On August 3, 1548, she gave birth to a daughter, Mary, only to die, like so many, of the complications of childbirth. Katherine was buried in St Mary's at Sudeley, which was sacked in the Civil War a century later. Her tomb features a marble effigy and the coats of arms of her four husbands. Less than a year after her death, Thomas Seymour, who had single-mindedly pursued Princess Elizabeth, was executed for "treason and other misdemeanours."

In Hertfordshire, the Old Palace at Hatfield House was acquired by Henry from the Bishop of Ely in an exchange. It was originally built around a courtyard; a fine brick wing remains. Henry used the palace to house his children, safely distant from court. Elizabeth spent a happy childhood there and shared in her young half-brother's education. It was to Hatfield that her half-sister, Mary, was humiliatingly sent by Anne Boleyn, to wait upon her. Here, too, Elizabeth was kept under virtual house arrest upon Mary's accession. She is said to have been sitting under an oak in the park in 1558 when news reached her of Mary's death and her own accession to the throne.

The Vyne in Hampshire is where Lord Chamberlain William Sandys played host to Henry and Anne Boleyn. Acton Court in Gloucestershire recalls the extravagance of Sir Nicholas Poyntz, who spent a fortune to receive the couple on a summer progress.

Of Cardinal Wolsey no trace remains. He was buried at Leicester Abbey, which came crashing down in the Dissolution of the Monasteries. This was not how he had planned it. His sarcophagus, as we have seen, is in the Nelson Chamber in the crypt of St Paul's.

England is littered with reminders of the vandalism of Henry VIII's Dissolution of the Monasteries. The shattered abbeys of Rievaulx, Jervaulx, and Whitby in North Yorkshire, Tintern in Monmouthshire, and Glastonbury in Somerset appear romantic and evocative to our eyes. In the wake of the destruction, when all was raw hurt and trauma, they were hideous scars on the landscape.

In the names of stately homes, also, we hear echoes of the Dissolution. Newstead Abbey in Nottingham would become the seat of the poet George Gordon, Lord Byron, his "Gothic Babel of a thousand years," to quote his poem *Don Juan*; he dug up the floor in the north cloister in a mad search for monastic gold. Woburn Abbey, where the last abbot, Robert Hobbes, was hanged in 1538 for failing to preach Henry's supremacy, bears no resemblance

ABOVE: *The series of artillery forts commissioned by Henry to protect England's vulnerable shores against invasion stands as part of his legacy. Deal Castle in Kent, was built to the design of a double cloverleaf or Tudor rose. Some say that Anne of Cleves stayed a night here on the way to meet her future husband.*

today to the 12th-century Cistercian monastery snatched by Thomas Cromwell's men. A gift from Henry to the 1st Earl of Bedford, and rebuilt for the 4th Duke in the mid-18th century, it opened its doors to the paying public in 1955; the showman 13th Duke watched his first visitors arrive that day in two cars and astride a bicycle.

Reminders of Henry's alienation from his continental cousins exist in his device forts, a series of artillery fortifications raised to defend England's south coast against invasion. Deal Castle in Kent is built to a perfect Tudor rose or double-cloverleaf design; within, it is soulless. Next-door Walmer Castle became the official residence of the Lord Warden of the Cinque Ports, including the Duke of Wellington, who died there with his boots off.

At Sandgate Castle in Kent and Camber Castle in East Sussex we may see the work of Stefan von Haschenperg, eccentric military engineer and "gentleman of Moravia." In the far north, he was employed in shoring up the red-stone Carlisle Castle, before being sacked for having "lewdly behaved himself and spent a great treasure to no purpose." He wrote from Antwerp seeking Henry's favor, with a scheme for bringing fresh water to Nonsuch Palace, "an art unknown to Vitruvius, Archimedes and Ctesibius, a horse-driven water pumping mill, a marvel fit for 'Non-Such' Palace." The marvel did not materialize.

☞ All is vanity

For two days, Henry's death was kept a secret from the public while the Privy Council made arrangements for a smooth succession and tinkered with his will to their great profit.

Back in 1518, when he was still in love with his Spanish queen, the king had engaged the Italian sculptor Pietro Torrigiano to produce designs for the tomb that they would share. Torrigiano was the creator of Henry's parents' magnificent monument in Westminster Abbey. For Henry and Katharine there was to be a bigger, better one, in the same white marble and black stone. However, artist and patron fell out over money, and the sculptor left England the following year.

One of Torrigiano's countrymen, Jacopo Sansovino, was later called upon to draw up a plan for "the Tombe to be made for the King's Grace at Windsore." It was to be a monumental edifice with life-sized effigies of Jane Seymour and Henry, gilded bronze angels, white marble pillars topped with figures of the apostles, and an equestrian statue of the king under a triumphal arch ("of the whole stature of a goodly man and a large horse"). No fewer than 134 figures were to be represented, including those of John the Baptist and St George, "all of brass gilt as in the pattern appeareth."

In his will Henry decreed that his body be taken to Windsor for temporary interment in a vault under the Quire at St George's Chapel, where Jane Seymour was buried. Their remains were to be reburied together when the monument was completed.

However, just as, in life, he had lost all vestige of dignity, so it was in death. There are reports that as his solemn funeral procession rested overnight at Syon House in Middlesex on its way from Whitehall Palace, his coffin exploded. More probably, its huge weight caused it to fall and break open.

In any event, somehow the money or the impetus was lacking to fulfill his scheme for his magnificent last resting place. He lies with Jane in St George's Chapel, Windsor, beneath a marble slab laid in 1837. With them, as the inscription tells, lie two later incumbents, the beheaded Charles I and an infant child of Queen Anne's. Oliver Cromwell ordered the removal of the executed Charles to Windsor, where Henry's unmarked tomb was rediscovered and put to further purpose.

The first Renaissance-style equestrian statue in England, by the French sculptor Hubert Le Sueur, stands on a tall plinth in Trafalgar Square and seems to want to gallop down Whitehall to reclaim Parliament. It is not of Henry but of that other king discarded with him—Charles I cuts a figure Henry could only dream of. London has but one outdoor statue of Henry VIII. It stands in a niche above the gateway to St Bartholomew's Hospital, known as "Bart's." One might easily fail to notice it, but still it is more than he deserves.

One adverse side effect of the suppression of the monasteries was that hospitals were often taken down with them. Many towns and cities had no hospital at all. In London, Bart's barely survived the closure of St Bartholomew-the-Great priory church. Sir Richard Gresham, the Lord Mayor, wrote to Henry to beg that London's few hospitals still standing be placed, with their revenues, at his and his aldermen's disposal. His appeal to the squeamish, plague-phobic king that the sick and blind and lame were lying about the streets, "offending every clean person passing by with their filthy and nasty savour," found no royal response. Finally, in 1546, the king granted the hospital to the City of London in consideration of an annual payment of 500 marks for its maintenance. The contract between Henry and the City, with his Great Seal, can be seen in the museum located in the north wing of this hospital—the oldest hospital in Britain to stand on its original site, and of which Henry is erroneously named as "founder."

ABOVE: *London's sole public statue of Henry VIII stands in a niche over the entrance gate to St Bartholomew's Hospital in West Smithfield. It was erected in 1702. Henry himself would have hoped for something far grander; many would say it is more than he deserved.*

RIGHT: *A half sovereign from the brief reign of the boy king Edward VI. The Gold Sovereign, official coinage of the English monarchy, was first minted in honor of Henry VII in 1489. The name fell into disuse in the reign of Elizabeth I, when the 20-shilling gold coin became known as the pound.*

✒ Of shoes and ships and sealing wax

In September 1547 commissioners were appointed to draw up an inventory of Henry's movable goods. Taking 18 months to compile, it listed everything from ships to spectacles, and included munitions, tents, horses, armor, 2,000 tapestries, 2,250 pieces of plate, books, paintings, clocks, masque costumes, robes, jewels, cloths of silver and gold…

Henry loved his treasures and fine threads, but nothing on earth had higher value to him than his heir. Edward was nine at his father's death. Henry had decided that a council of regency should rule on his behalf, but, as with his tomb, what he ordained he could no longer enforce. Edward's uncle, Edward Seymour, took control as the Duke of Somerset and Lord Protector, supported by Archbishop Cranmer and John Dudley, Earl of Warwick.

The power struggles that resulted in Edward Seymour joining his brother and the other illustrious souls beneath the Tower chapel are not to be told here. Young Edward VI, never strong, died in July 1553, in his 16th year, and with him died the Tudor kings' male lineage.

ABOVE: *Dating from 1546 and attributed to the Netherlander William Scrots, this portrait of Princess Elizabeth, the future Elizabeth I, like that of her half-brother, Edward, was probably painted for her father. "The outwarde shadow of the body" was how she described a portrait of herself that she sent to Edward; we see here that she dwells in her "inwarde minde."*

When Henry's daughter Mary came to the throne, aged 37, she was committed to the restoration of the Catholic faith. She married Philip of Spain, who was the son of her cousin Charles V and was 16 years her junior. Their union was a disaster, a single "pregnancy" turned out to be a phantom, and, with Boulogne already relinquished in Edward's reign, England's last foothold in France, Calais, was lost. Mary's half-sister, Elizabeth, who succeeded her to the throne, never married and had no issue.

It is a fitting postscript to the great Greek tragedy that was the life of Henry VIII that the Tudor royal dynasty simply died out. Henry had wanted everything he could take from life, in wealth, in glory, in prestige, in love and lust and progeny and posterity. The inventory of his worldly goods ran to hundreds of thousands of items. And yet in the final reckoning he was left with absolutely nothing.

There was, though, in a sense, a happy ending to this tale, in the many glories of the reign of Elizabeth I. She ascended the throne in 1558, aged 25, and ruled England until 1603. This really was, in many ways, a golden age: the glory days of Shakespeare, Spenser, Marlowe, Ben Jonson, Philip Sidney. These were years of exploration and adventure, of Sir Francis Drake's voyage around the world. Sir Walter Raleigh discovered Guiana; he established the Virginia colony of Roanoke Island. His half-brother Humphrey Gilbert discovered Newfoundland. Drake's second cousin Sir John Hawkins sailed to West Africa and South America.

Some of England's most beautiful country houses date from the high Elizabethan era, including Longleat House in Wiltshire, Hardwick Hall (the many large windows of which led to the contemporary rhyme "Hardwick Hall, more window than wall") in Derbyshire, Burghley House in Lincolnshire, and Wollaton Hall in Nottingham.

Theater became a national pastime. Indeed, court life was an art form in itself. There were plots and intrigues, there was persecution, but Anne Boleyn's daughter emerges as one of the best-known and most successful sovereigns in English history.

The concubine and the bastard did very well indeed.

FURTHER READING

Account of Revels. &c. drawn up by Richard Gibson at the King's order
www.british-history.ac.uk/report.aspx?compid=90986

The Book of the Courtier by Count Baldesar Castiglione
archive.org/stream/bookofcourtier00castuoft/bookofcourtier00castuoft_djvu.txt

British History Online, Letters and Papers of Henry VIII, Foreign and Domestic
www.british-history.ac.uk/catalogue.aspx?gid=126

Coronation Ode of King Henry VIII by Thomas More
thomasmorestudies.org/docs/Mores_1509_Coronation_Ode.pdf

The Fifth Queen: And How She Came to Court, a novel by Ford Madox Ford.
www.gutenberg.org/files/30188/30188-h/30188-h.htm

Holinshed's Chronicles of England, Scotland and Ireland
www.gutenberg.org/files/42506/42506-h/42506-h.htm

The Life and Death of Cardinal Wolsey by George Cavendish
archive.org/stream/lifeanddeathofca027728mbp#page/n21/mode/2up

Love Letters of Henry VIII to Anne Boleyn
www.gutenberg.org/files/32155/32155-h/32155-h.htm

The Noble Tryumphaunt Coronacyon of Quene Anne – Wyfe unto the Noble Kynge Henry the Viii, Wynkin de Worde
www.oocities.org/coronation_book/3.htm

The Privy Purse Expenses of King Henry the Eighth from November 1529 to December 1532
archive.org/stream/henryprivypurse00nicouoft/henryprivypurse00nicouoft_djvu.txt

Selected Works of John Skelton
www.luminarium.org/renlit/skelbib.htm

Tudor Constitutional Documents
archive.org/stream/cu31924030504322/cu31924030504322_djvu.txt

The Works of Henry VIII
www.luminarium.org/renlit/tudorbib.htm

INDEX

Page numbers in *italic* refer to captions

Act of Succession 96
Act of Suppression 148
Act of Supremacy 96–97, 112
Acton Court 43, 181
Anne of Cleves, Queen of England 140, 142–143, 150, 153–154, 167
appearance 142
death of 180

divorce 153
Henry's reaction to 132, 140, 143, 150
hopes for reinstatement 167
portraits *140*
precontract with Francis of Lorraine 143
rumoured pregnancy 167
as stepmother 155
"the king's good sister" 153, 155

Anne of Cleves House 179–180, *180*
apothecaries 175
armour *171, 173*
Arthur, Prince of Wales 17, 18, *18*, 180
artillery forts 182
Aske, Robert 168
astrology 17, 96, 110

Bacon, Francis 31
barber surgeons *165*, 175

barbers 52
Baynard's Castle 39, *39*, 178
Baynton, Sir Edward 107
Beaufort, Lady Margaret (Countess of Richmond and Derby) 17, 18
Becket, Thomas 148–149
Bedford, John Russell, 1st Earl of 120
bedmaking ritual, royal 6
Bigod, Sir Francis 146

Blount, Elizabeth (Bessie) 36, 38, 49

Blount, John 36

Boleyn, Anne, Queen of England 7, 8, 38, 60–65, 70, 83, 86, 90, 93, 98, *115*, 137, 159, 166, 179
  accomplishments 66, *66*
  appearance 60–61
  arrest and imprisonment 93, 107–108, *108*
  betrothal to Henry Percy 64–65
  birth and early life 60
  burial of 115
  clothes 62, 63, 64, 95, 108
  coronation 95, *96*
  created Marquess of Pembroke 94
  downfall 107–108, 121
  execution of 108
  Henry's courtship of 62–63
  hostility to Katharine and Mary 101, 103, *103*, 104
  hostility to Wolsey 65, 82, 86
  marries Henry 94
  miscarriages 107, 164
  portraits *61*, *62*, *82*, *101*
  pregnancies 95, 103, 107
  Reformist religious views 98
  trial 120–121
  unpopularity 95

Boleyn, George, Viscount Rochford 8, 69, 108, 150, 179

Boleyn, Mary 38, 60

Boleyn, Sir Thomas 38, 38, 103, 151, 154

The Book of the Courtier (Castiglione) 65–66, 127

Boorde, Andrew 161, 162

Bosworth, Battle of (1485) 17, 162

Boulogne, siege of (1544) 171

Bowes, Sir Martin 112, 115

Brereton, William 108

Bridewell Palace 39, 178

Bryan, Sir Francis 49, 51, 53, 118, 121

Buckingham, Edward Stafford, 3rd Duke of 43, 179

Burghley House 185

Butts, Sir William 49, 175, *175*

Byron, Lord George 181

Camber Castle 182

Campeggio, Lorenzo 84

Canterbury Cathedral 148–149, *149*

Carew, Sir Nicholas 49, *49*, 51, 53, 118, 121, 132, 147

Carles, Lancelot de 61

Carlisle Castle 182

Castiglione, Count Baldassare 65–66, *65*

Castillon, Louis de Perreau, Sieur de 134, 135, 139, 164

Cavendish, George *46*, 65, 73, 77–78, 82, 86, 89, 90, 125–126

Chambers, John *174*, 175

Chapuys, Eustace 100–101, 103, 104, 106–107, 118, 120, 137, 143, 159, 162, 164, 167, 171

Charles I 183

Charles II *39*

Charles V, Holy Roman Emperor 26, 31, 42, 100, *104*, 106, 132, 135, 137, 139, 143, 185

Charles, Duke of Orléans *112*

Chelsea Old Manor 180

Chertsey Abbey 155

Chieregato, Francesco 35

Christina of Denmark, Duchess of Milan 135, *136*, 138–139

clocks *64*, *179*

clothes and jewels 56, 58–59, 62, 63–64, 95, 108, 135

coinage 112, 115, 184
  debasement of 112

Columbus, Christopher 42

Compton, Sir William 49, *50*, 51, 52, 53

Compton Wynyates *50*, 51

Cornysh, William 24, 29, 30, 31

courtiers, model 65–66, 127

courtly love 66, 70

Cranmer, Thomas, Archbishop of Canterbury 77, 94, 118, 156–157, 172, 178, 179, 184

Cromwell, Oliver 183

Cromwell, Thomas, Earl of Essex 46, 53, 96, 104, 121, 129, 132, 134, 137–138, 139, 140, 143, 146–147, *146*, 148, 149, 150, 154, 155, 179

Culpeper, Thomas 155, 156, 158, 159

Deal Castle 182, *182*

Dereham, Francis 153, 158

Dissolution of the Monasteries 112, 115, 118, 145, 148–149, 178, 181, 184

Drake, Sir Francis 185

Dudley, Edmund 31, 166

Dürer, Albrecht *166*

Duwes, Gilles 24

Edward IV 56, 59, 175

Edward V 18, 110

Edward VI *126*, 128, *128*, 137, 165, 169, 181, *183*, 184

Elizabeth of York, Queen of England 16, 17, 18, 20, *20*, 128

Elizabeth, Princess (later, Elizabeth I) 95, *96*, 100, 101, 103, *126*, 128, 137, 165, 181, 185, *185*

Eltham Ordinances 46, 48–49, 51, 52–53, 122, 123

Eltham Palace 39, 179

Empson, Richard 31, 166

Erasmus, Desiderius 22, 38, 137, 140, 166, 179

Esquires of the Body 36, 38, 56

Exeter Conspirators (1538) 146–147

Ferdinand II of Aragon 14, 18, 20

Ferrers, Walter Devereux, Lord 7

Field of Cloth of Gold (1520) 30, 31, *33*, 38, 79

Fisher, John, Bishop of Rochester 98, 138, *138*, 179

FitzRoy, Henry, Duke of Richmond and Somerset 36, *36*, 38, 118, 179

Flodden, Battle of (1513) 36

food and feasts 45, 117, 118, 121–126

Fools 26, *27*, *126*
football 26
Francis I of France 30–31, 36, 38, 51, 56, *59*, 132, 134, 135, 139, 143, 178
French hoods 62, *66*, 83
Fulbroke Castle 51
Fuller, Thomas 121

Gainsborough Old Hall *157*
gambling 7, 22, 26
gardens 89–90
garderobes 88
Gardiner, Stephen, Bishop of Winchester 172
Gentlemen Ushers 6
Gibson, Richard 28, 30, 36, 38
Gilbert, Humphrey 185
Gilbert, Sir John *78*
girdle books *108*
Giustiniani, Sebastian 30, 56, 164
A Glass of the Truthe (Henry VIII) 88
Glastonbury Abbey 145, *148*
Greenwich Palace (Palace of Placentia) *16*, 39, 121, 126, 178
Gresham, Sir Richard 184
Grey, Lady Jane 179
Grooms of the Bedchamber 6
Grooms of the Stool 49, 53, 88, 108
Guildford, Sir Henry 38

Hampton Court 74, 77–78, 79, 82, 86–87, 88–90, *91*, *94*, 118, 125, 179
astronomical clock 179, *179*

Chapel Royal 77
gardens 89–90
Great Hall 87, *87*
hauntings 179
kitchens 121–122, *122*
Hardwick Hall 185
Harrison, William 146
Haschenperg, Stefan von 182
Hatfield House 181
hawking *26*
Hawkins, Sir John 185
Henry III 112
Henry VII 16, 17, 18, 20, 22, 22, 31
Henry VIII
accession 14, 16, 22
appearance 56, 59, 171
birth and early life 16–17
character and temperament 59, 164, 166
clothes and jewels 56, 59, 60, 135
death of 178, 182
Defender of the Faith 88, 100, 112
education and accomplishments 17, 24–25
excommunication 139
at Field of Cloth of Gold 30, 31, *33*
foreign policies 31, 79, 143
and the Great Matter 79, 82, 83–85, 88
health concerns and physical decline 118, 155, 162, 164–166, *165*, 171, 174, 175
horoscope 17, *17*
illegitimate children 38

inventory of worldly goods 184, 185
letters of 55, 63, *63*
marries Anne Boleyn 94
marries Anne of Cleves 143
marries Jane Seymour 108
marries Katharine of Aragon 22
marries Katherine Parr 167
marries Kathryn Howard 155
military campaigns 26, 36, 169–170, 171
musical composition 24–25, *25*
portraits *14*, *56*, 58, *118*, *126*, *132*, 137, *162*, *164*
as Prince of Wales 14, 20
relations with Charles V 26, 31, 42, 139
relations with Francis I 30–31, 134, 135
religious beliefs and writings *45*, 87–88, 172
sports and pastimes 6, 26–27, 90, 156, 164
Supreme Head of the Church of England 96
tomb of 182–183
virility 49, 51, 150, 166, *175*
will and testament 177, 182, 183
Hever Castle *42*, 44, 154, *154*, 179
Hogarth, William 84
Holbein, Hans 58, *61*, *70*, *97*, *104*, *118*, *121*, *129*, 131, *132*, *136*, 137–139, 140, 142, *146*, *164*, 175

Horenbout, Lucas *14*, *60*, *83*, 137
horoscope 17, *17*
hospitals 184
Howard, Catherine (daughter of 2nd Duke of Norfolk, wife of Rhys ap Gruffydd) 7
Howard, Henry see Surrey, Henry Howard, Earl of
Howard, Kathryn 8, 9, 77, 150–151, 153, *153*, 155, 156–159, 179
adultery 155, 156, 158
birth and early life 150–151
early love affairs 151, 153
execution of 159
Howard, Thomas *see* Norfolk, Thomas Howard, 3rd Duke of
humors, doctrine of the 164
hunting 6, 90
Huntly, George Gordon, 4th Earl of 170
Hutton, John 135, 138, 139, 146

Isabella I of Castile 18, 42

James IV of Scotland 18, 36
James V of Scotland 132, 156, 169
John, King 112
John III, Duke of Cleves 140
jousting 26–27, *28*, 40, 49, 90, 118, 164

Katharine of Aragon, Queen of England 7, 9, 14, 22, 24, 36, 38, 59, 60, 63, 64, 77, 86, *91*, 103, 120, 180
acts as regent 36

Anne Boleyn's hostility toward 104
appearance 14
death and burial of 106–107
lives away from the court 46, 100–101
marriage annulment 79, 83–84, 94
marriage to Arthur, Prince of Wales 18, 20, 84
portraits *18*, *60*
pregnancies and children 29, 30, 36
Kell/McLeod hypothesis 166
Kimbolton Castle 100, 106, 180
King's College of Physicians 174–175
Knights of the Garter 56, 58, 125
Knole House 179
knot gardens 89–90, *89*

Lascelles, John 156, 157
Latimer, John Neville, 3rd Baron 168, 169
Le Sueur, Hubert 183
Leeds Castle 179
Leicester Abbey 90, 181
Leo X, Pope 88, 112
Linacre, Thomas 175
Longleat House 185
Louis XII of France 18, 60, 79
Ludlow Castle 20, 83, 180
Lutheranism 87, 100, 154

magnificence, requirement for 6, 30, 45, 78–79, 123
Maiano, Giovanni da 75
makeup 66, 120

male hierarchical society 59
Mallard, Jean 24
Mannox, Henry 151, 153, 157–158
Margaret of Austria, Duchess of Savoy 22
Margaret Tudor, Queen of Scotland 18
Marguerite of Valois 134, 139
Marillac, Charles de 154, 155, 156, 158, 159, 162
Mary of Guise, Queen of Scotland 132, 134, *134*, 135, 169
Mary, Princess (later, Queen of England) 8, 36, 83, *83*, 91, 100, 101, 103, *103*, 104, 126–127, *126*, 128, 137, 165, 166, 181, 185
Mary, Queen of Scots 169, 170
Mary Tudor, Queen of France 18, 60, 79
masques and pageants 14, 27, 28–30, 36, 166
medicine 164, 174–175
Memo, Friar Dionisius 24
The More 91, 100
More, Alice 98
More, Sir Thomas 13, 16, 96–98, *97*, 100, 115, 137, 179
Mountjoy, William Blount, 4th Baron 14, 16, 36
music 24–25, *24*, *25*, 66, *66*

Navy 41, 178
Nelson, Lord 90
Neville, Sir Edward 146
Newstead Abbey 181
Nonsuch Palace 178, *178*, 182

Norfolk, Agnes, Duchess of 150, 151, 153, 157–158
Norfolk, Thomas Howard, 3rd Duke of 7–8, 104, *104*, 106, 108, 138, 143, 146, 154, 158, 172
Norris, Sir Henry 53, 88, 108, 112
Northumberland, Henry Percy, 5th Earl of 64, 65

Oatlands Palace 155
Opicijs, Benedictus de 24
Oursian, Nicholas 179
Owen, George 175

pageboys 52
Palace of Placentia *see* Greenwich Palace
Palace of Westminster 39
palaces 39, 178–181
see also individual index entries
Parr, Katherine, Queen of England 9, 167–169, 170–172, 174, 180, 181
acts as regent 171
earlier marriages 168
marries Seymour 181
portrait *170*
Reformist religious views 171–172
as stepmother 170
Parron, William 17
Partridge, Sir Miles 26
patronage 46, 52, 69
Paul III, Pope 98, 139
Penshurst Place 43–44, *44*, 179
Percy, Henry (later, 6th Earl of Northumberland) 64–65
Peterborough Cathedral 9, 107, 180
Philip of Spain 185

physicians 174–175
Pilgrimage of Grace (1536–37) 115, 127, 168, 171
Pio da Carpi, Rodolfo 38
plague 43, 79
poetry 69, 70
Pole, Sir Geoffrey 146
Pole, Cardinal Reginald 146–147, 148
Popincourt, Jane 38
Poyntz, Sir Nicholas 43, *43*, 181
praemunire 86
Prebendaries Plot (1543) 172
Privy Chamber 45–46, 49, 51–53, 108, 124
prodigy houses 79
progresses 42–44, 90, 155–156

Raleigh, Sir Walter 185
Raphael 65, *65*
Reformation 100, 148
Revels Office 27, 28
Rhys ap Gruffydd 7, 8
Richard III 17, 18, 110
Richmond Palace 22, 39, 89, 91, 178
Robin Hood 14, 28, 31
Rochford, Lady Jane 150, 158, 159
Roper, Meg 97, 98
Rough Wooing 170
Rovezzano, Benedetto da 75
Rowlett, Ralph 115
royal household
management 44–45, 46
Black Book 44
Eltham Ordinances 46, 48–49, 51, 52–53, 122, 123

privy purse expenses 7
Royal Mint 112, 115

Sadler, Sir Ralph *151*
St Bartholomew's Hospital 183, 184, *184*
St George's Chapel, Windsor 183
St James's Palace 179
St Paul's Cathedral 90
Salisbury, Margaret Pole, Countess of 147–148
Sander, Nicholas 60, 62–63
Sandgate Castle 182
Sandys, William, 1st Baron 44, 91, 106, 108, 181
sanitation 49, 88
Sansovino, Jacopo 183
Scarpinello, Augustino 86
Scotland 36, 169–170, 171
Seymour, Sir Edward *see* Somerset, Edward Seymour, Duke of
Seymour, Jane, Queen of England 107, 120–121, 126–127, 179, 183
appearance 120
death of 128
Henry interred with 183
kindness to Princess Mary 126–127
portraits *121, 126*
pregnancy and birth of son 126, 127, 128
Seymour, Sir John 120
Seymour, Sir Thomas (later, Lord Sudeley) 120, *168*, 169, 172, 180, 181
Sharp, John 49
Shelton, Anne 103
Shelton, Margaret (Madge) 103, 120, 135

Shrewsbury, George Talbot, 3rd Earl of 64, 122
Sittow, Michael 22
Skelton, John 17, 52, 69–70, 74, 77
Skutt, John 63
smallpox 42, 142, 164
Smeaton, Mark 24, 108
Solway Moss, Battle of (1542) 169
Somers, Will *26, 27, 126, 173*
Somerset, Edward Seymour, Duke of (earlier, Earl of Hertford) 120, 121, 128, 170, *183*, 184
sports and pastimes 26–27, 66, 90, 156, 164
Sudeley Castle *168*, 180–181
sumptuary laws 56, 58–59, 124–125
superstitions 110
Surrey, Henry Howard, Earl of 8, 69, *69*
Sutton House *151*
sweating sickness 20, 53, 82–83, 162
syphilis 42, 162, 164–165, *166*

tag rhyming 26
Tallis, Thomas 24
tapestries 74–75, *87*
taxation 6, 31
tennis 26, 66, 164
Thames, River 40–41, *41*
Thomas, William 49
Torrigiano, Pietro 88, 182
Toto del Nunziata, Antonio 88
Tower of London 39, 94–95, 110–112, 115, 158

Bell Tower 98, *98*
Chapel of St Peter ad Vincula 115, *159*, 179
Royal Menagerie 110, 112
Traitor's Gate *115*
White Tower 110, *111, 112*
trade 41–42
Treasons Act 97, 175
Treaty of Windsor (1522) 31
Tusser, Thomas 90
Tyler, William 49
Tyndale, William 98

uprisings 146
see also Pilgrimage of Grace

Vicary, Thomas *165*, 175
The Vyne 44, 91, 106, 181

Waldegrave, Edward 153, 158
Walmer Castle 182
Waltham Abbey 149
Warham, William, Archbishop of Canterbury 138
Warwick, John Dudley, Earl of 184
Wellington, Duke of 182
Westminster Abbey 22, 95, 182
Weston, Sir Francis 108
Whitehall Palace 86, 178
Whiting, Richard *148*
Wilder, Philip van 25
Windsor Castle 39, 128, 179
witchcraft 110
Woburn Abbey 181–182
Wollaton Hall 185

Wolsey, Thomas 46, 51–52, 53, 64, 69, 73, 74–75, 77, 78–79, *78*, 89, 122, 125, 162
death and burial of 90, 181
Eltham ordinances 46, 48–49, 51, 52–53, 122, 123
and the Great Matter 79, 82, 84
ill health 74, *75*
illegitimate children 77
portraits *46, 78*
praemunire charge 86
relationship with Anne Boleyn 65, 82, 86
relationship with Henry 74, 77, 79, 82, 85–86
rise to power 46
wealth 74–75, 77, 78
Worde, Wynkyn de 95, 117, *123, 124*
Wotton, Nicholas 140, 142, 143
Wriothesley, Sir Thomas 135, 139, 142
Wyatt, George 61–62
Wyatt, Sir Thomas 61, *69*, 70, 139

Yeomen of the Bedchamber 6
Yeomen of the Body 36
Yeomen of the Wardrobe 6
York, Richard, Duke of 18, 110
York Place 64, 79, 86

PICTURE CREDITS

VIII, late 16th century (oil on panel), Holbein the Younger, Hans (1497/8-1543) (after) / Royal Armouries, Leeds, UK; page 134 Alamy/ © GL Archive; page 136 Alamy/ © GL Archive; page 138 Bridgeman Images/John Fisher, Bishop of Rochester, c.1532-34 (black & coloured chalks, brown wash, pen, brush and ink on paper), Holbein the Younger, Hans (1497/8-1543) / Royal Collection Trust © Her Majesty Queen Elizabeth II, 2014; page 141 Corbis/© The Gallery Collection; page 147 Alamy/ © Image Asset Management Ltd; page 148 Alamy/ © Anthony Collins; page149 Alamy/ © Art Directors & TRIP; page 151 Alamy/ © The National Trust Photolibrary; page152 Getty Images/The Bridgeman Art Library; page154 Getty Images/The Bridgeman Art Library; 157 Getty Images/The Bridgeman Art Library; 159 Alamy/ © Peter Carroll; page163 The Art Archive; page 165 Alamy/ © North Wind Picture Archives; page 166 Alamy/ © INTERFOTO; page 168 Alamy/ © Krzysztof Melech;

page 170 Getty Images/De Agostini; page 171 Alamy/ © Marco Secchi; page 173 Corbis/© Heritage Images; page 174 Kunsthistorisches Museum Vienna; page 175 Alamy/ © Heritage Image Partnership Ltd; page 178 Alamy/The Art Gallery Collection; page 179 Alamy/ IMAGES; page 180 Alamy/ © Tony Lilley; page 181 Bridgeman Images/Locket ring belonging to Queen Elizabeth I, c.1575 (gold with enamel, rubies, diamonds & mother-of-pearl), English School, (16th century) / By Kind Permission of the Chequers Trust / Photo © Mark Fiennes; page 182 Corbis/ © Skyscan; page 183 Getty Images/The Bridgeman Art Library; page 184 top Getty Images/UIG; page 184 bottom Getty Images/UIG; page 185 Corbis.

Every effort has been made to contact copyright holders and acknowledge sources. Any omissions will be rectified in future printings, if brought to the publisher's attention.

Acknowledgments

It has been such a pleasure to work on this book with Penny Craig and Alison Wormleighton, consummate editor and brilliantly incisive copy editor respectively. I would also like to thank publisher Cindy Richards, whose idea this book was originally. Grateful thanks, also, to Claire Gouldstone for bringing the pictures together, to Becca Thorne for providing the illustrations, and to David Rowley and Sally Powell for such a fun design. And finally thanks to Patricia Harrington for the production of a fine-looking book.